First World War
and Army of Occupation
War Diary
France, Belgium and Germany

51 DIVISION
Divisional Troops
255 Brigade Royal Field Artillery
1 June 1915 - 31 March 1919

WO95/2854/3

The Naval & Military Press Ltd
www.nmarchive.com
Published in association with The National Archives

Published by

The Naval & Military Press Ltd

Unit 10 Ridgewood Industrial Park,

Uckfield, East Sussex,

TN22 5QE England

Tel: +44 (0) 1825 749494

www.naval-military-press.com

www.nmarchive.com

This diary has been reprinted in facsimile from the original. Any imperfections are inevitably reproduced and the quality may fall short of modern type and cartographic standards.

© **Crown Copyright**
Images reproduced by permission of The National Archives, London, England, 2015.

Contents

Document type	Place/Title	Date From	Date To
Heading	WO95/2854/3 255 Brigade Royal Field Artillery 1915 June 1919 March		
Heading	51st Division 255th (Highland) Bde RFA Jun 1915-Mar 1919		
Heading	51st Division 1/1 Highland Bde RFA Vol I. 1-30.6.15		
War Diary	In The Field	01/06/1915	30/06/1915
Heading	51st Division 1/1 Highland Bde RFA Vol II From 1st To 30th July 1915		
War Diary	In The Field	01/07/1915	30/07/1915
Heading	51st Division 1/1 Highland Bde RFA. Vol III From 1-31-8-15		
War Diary	In The Field	01/08/1915	31/08/1915
Heading	51st Division 1/1 Highland Bde. R.F.A. Vol IV Sep 15		
War Diary	In The Field	01/09/1915	30/09/1915
Heading	51st Division 1/1 Highland R.F.A. Bde. Oct-15 Vol V		
War Diary	In the field	01/10/1915	25/10/1915
Heading	51st Division 1/1 Highland R.F.A. Bde. Nov 1915 Vol VI		
War Diary	Field	01/11/1915	30/11/1915
Heading	51st Division 1/1 Highland Bde. R.F.A. Dec 1915 Vol VII		
War Diary	Field	01/12/1915	31/12/1915
Heading	1st Bde R.F.A. Jan 1916 Vol VIII		
War Diary	Field	05/01/1916	31/01/1916
War Diary	St. Sauveur	01/02/1916	01/02/1916
War Diary	Bussy Les Daours	07/02/1916	20/02/1916
War Diary	Bray	22/02/1916	28/02/1916
War Diary	Villers Bocage	29/02/1916	29/02/1916
War Diary	Field	01/03/1916	31/03/1916
War Diary	Fond De Vase Near Maroeuil	01/04/1916	30/04/1916
War Diary	Field Fond De Vase Near Maroeuil	01/05/1916	21/05/1916
War Diary	Fond De Vase Near Maroeuil	21/05/1916	31/05/1916
War Diary	Fond De Vase	01/06/1916	30/06/1916
Heading	War Diary Of 253rd Brigade R.F.A. From 1st July 1916 To 31st July 1916 Vol 14		
War Diary	Fond De Vase	01/07/1916	31/07/1916
Heading	51st Division Artillery. 255th Brigade Royal Field Artillery August 1916		
War Diary		01/08/1916	31/08/1916
Heading	War Diary of 255th (High) Brigade R.F.A.T 1st Sept 1916 To 30th Sept 1916		
War Diary	Armentieres	01/09/1916	23/09/1916
War Diary	Caudescure	24/09/1916	25/09/1916
War Diary	Raimbert	26/09/1916	26/09/1916
War Diary	Bergueneuse	27/09/1916	27/09/1916
War Diary	Vacquerie Le Boucq	28/09/1916	28/09/1916
War Diary	Bois Du Warnimont	29/09/1916	29/09/1916
War Diary	Pushvillers	29/09/1916	30/09/1916
War Diary	Mesnil	01/10/1916	06/10/1916
War Diary	Colincamps	07/10/1916	16/10/1916

War Diary	Mailly Maillet	17/10/1916	31/10/1916
Heading	War Diary of 255th (Highland) Brigade R.F.A.T. for month of October. 1916. Vol 17		
Operation(al) Order(s)	51st Divisional Artillery. Operation Order No. 58.	23/10/1916	23/10/1916
Heading	War Diary of 255th Brigade Royal Field Artillery From 1st November To 30th November 1916. Vol 18		
War Diary		01/11/1916	30/11/1916
Heading	War Diary of 255th (Highland) Brigade R.F.A.Y For the month of December 1916.		
War Diary	Courcelette	01/12/1916	31/12/1916
Heading	War Diary of 255th (Highland) Brigade R.F.A.T for the month of January 1917 Vol 20		
War Diary	Courcelette	01/01/1917	05/01/1917
War Diary	Sarton	06/01/1917	06/01/1917
War Diary	Gezaincourt	07/01/1917	07/01/1917
War Diary	Beavuoir Rivier	08/01/1917	08/01/1917
War Diary	Grand	09/01/1917	09/01/1917
War Diary	Laviers	10/01/1917	31/01/1917
Heading	War Diary of 255th Brigade R.F.A.T for Month of February 1917 vol 21		
War Diary	Grand Laviers	01/02/1917	08/02/1917
War Diary	Magnicourt	09/02/1917	19/02/1917
War Diary	Ourton	19/02/1917	28/02/1917
Heading	War Diary of 255th (High) Brigade R.F.A.Y for month of March 1917 Vol 22		
War Diary	Ourton	01/03/1917	31/03/1917
War Diary	Madagascar	31/03/1917	31/03/1917
Heading	War Diary of 255th Brigade R.F.A.T. for month of April 1917. Vol 23		
War Diary	Madgascar	01/04/1917	13/04/1917
War Diary	Pont Du Jour	14/04/1917	30/04/1917
Heading	War Diary of 255th (High) Bde R.F.A.Y for month of May 1917		
War Diary	Point Du Jour	01/05/1917	31/05/1917
Heading	War Diary of 255th (High) Bde R.F.A.Y. for month of June 1917		
War Diary	Point Du Jour	01/06/1917	19/06/1917
War Diary	Acq	20/06/1917	30/06/1917
Heading	War Diary of 255th Brigade R.F.A.T. for Month of October 1917		
War Diary	Canal Bank	01/10/1917	18/10/1917
War Diary	Poperinghe	19/10/1917	20/10/1917
War Diary	Acheux	21/10/1917	31/10/1917
Heading	War Diary of 255th Bde R.F.A.T. for Month of November 1917		
War Diary	Acheux	01/11/1917	01/11/1917
War Diary	Boiry St Martin	03/11/1917	05/11/1917
War Diary	Acheux	06/11/1917	06/11/1917
War Diary	Courcelles	14/11/1917	14/11/1917
War Diary	Bearlencourt	15/11/1917	15/11/1917
War Diary	Bus	17/11/1917	17/11/1917
War Diary	Havrincourt Wood	18/11/1917	20/11/1917
War Diary	Flesquieres	21/11/1917	30/11/1917
Heading	War Diary of 255th (Highland) Brigade R.F.A.Y. for month of December 1917. Vol 31		
War Diary	Flesquieres	01/12/1917	04/12/1917

War Diary	Grand Ravine	05/12/1917	11/12/1917
War Diary	Beaumetz	12/12/1917	12/12/1917
War Diary	Les Camera	12/12/1917	29/12/1917
Heading	War Diary of 255th (Highland) Bde. R.F.A.Y. for month of January 1918		
War Diary	Beavmetz	01/01/1918	22/01/1918
War Diary	Avesnes	23/01/1918	23/01/1918
War Diary	Mally Maillet	24/01/1918	24/01/1918
War Diary	Authie	25/01/1918	31/01/1918
Heading	War Diary of 255th (Highland) Bde. R.F.A.Y. for month of February 1918. Vol 33		
War Diary	Authie	01/02/1918	08/02/1918
War Diary	Bouzincourt	12/02/1918	13/02/1918
War Diary	Beaumetz	14/02/1918	28/02/1918
Heading	51st Division Artillery War Diary 255th Royal Field Artillery March 1918		
War Diary	Beaumetz	01/03/1918	21/03/1918
War Diary	Lebucquiere	22/03/1918	22/03/1918
War Diary	Fremicourt	23/03/1918	23/03/1918
War Diary	Riencourt	23/03/1918	23/03/1918
War Diary	Thilloy	24/03/1918	24/03/1918
War Diary	Achiet Le Petit	24/03/1918	24/03/1918
War Diary	Puiseaux	25/03/1918	25/03/1918
War Diary	Serre	25/03/1918	25/03/1918
War Diary	Fonquevillers	25/03/1918	25/03/1918
War Diary	Bienvillers	26/03/1918	27/03/1918
War Diary	La Souich	29/03/1918	29/03/1918
War Diary	Wail	31/03/1918	31/03/1918
War Diary	Beaumetz	01/03/1918	21/03/1918
War Diary	Lebucquiere	22/03/1918	22/03/1918
War Diary	Fremicourt	23/03/1918	23/03/1918
War Diary	Riencourt	23/03/1918	23/03/1918
War Diary	Thilloy	24/03/1918	24/03/1918
War Diary	Achiet Le Petit	24/03/1918	24/03/1918
War Diary	Puiseaux	25/03/1918	25/03/1918
War Diary	Serre	25/03/1918	25/03/1918
War Diary	Fonquevillers.	25/03/1918	25/03/1918
War Diary	Bienvillers	26/03/1918	27/03/1918
War Diary	La Souich	28/03/1918	29/03/1918
War Diary	Wail	31/03/1918	31/03/1918
Heading	51st Divisional Artillery War Diary 255th (Highland) Brigade Royal Field Artillery April 1918		
Heading	War Diary of 255th (Highland) Bde R.F.A.Y for month of April 1918.		
War Diary	Haillicourt	01/04/1918	03/04/1918
War Diary	Amettes	04/04/1918	08/04/1918
War Diary	Paradis	09/04/1918	10/04/1918
War Diary	Riez Du Vinage	11/04/1918	11/04/1918
War Diary	Busnes	12/04/1918	12/04/1918
War Diary	Pecleme	15/04/1918	30/04/1918
Heading	War Diary of 255th (High) Bde. R.F.A.Y. for month of May 1918. Vol 36		
War Diary	Lecleme	01/05/1918	31/05/1918
War Diary	War Diary Of 255th (Highland) Bde. R.F.A.Y. for month of June 1918. Vol 37		
War Diary	Lecleme	01/05/1918	04/05/1918

War Diary	Estree Cauchie	05/05/1918	06/05/1918
War Diary	Madagascar	16/05/1918	16/05/1918
War Diary	Roclincourt	17/05/1918	30/05/1918
Heading	Divisional Artillery 51st (Highland) Division. 255th Brigade R.F.A. July 1916		
Heading	War Diary Of 255th Bde. R.F.A.Y. for month of July 1918. Vol 38		
War Diary	Roclincourt	01/07/1918	13/07/1918
War Diary	La Comte	16/07/1918	16/07/1918
War Diary	Pernes	15/07/1918	15/07/1918
War Diary	La Chapelle	16/07/1918	16/07/1918
War Diary	Clamanges	18/07/1918	18/07/1918
War Diary	Bois Le St Quentin	19/07/1918	23/07/1918
War Diary	Nahteuil La Pusse	24/07/1918	27/07/1918
War Diary	Pourcy	28/07/1918	28/07/1918
War Diary	St Imoges	30/07/1918	30/07/1918
War Diary	Epernay	31/07/1918	31/07/1918
Heading	War Diary of 255th (Highland) Bde. R.F.A.Y. For Month Of August 1918.		
War Diary	Acq	01/08/1918	14/08/1918
War Diary	Oclincourt	15/08/1918	21/08/1918
War Diary	Bois De La Maison Blanche	23/08/1918	23/08/1918
War Diary	Maison Blanche	23/08/1918	27/08/1918
War Diary	Musketry Valley	28/08/1918	31/08/1918
Heading	War Diary of 255th (Highland) Brigade R.F.A.T. for month of September, 1918. Vol 40		
War Diary	Musketry Valley	01/09/1918	06/09/1918
War Diary	Cam Valley	11/09/1918	12/09/1918
War Diary	Acq	13/09/1918	19/09/1918
War Diary	Cam Valley	24/09/1918	30/09/1918
Heading	War Diary of 255th (Highland) Bde R.F.A.Y. for month of October, 1918. Vol 41		
War Diary	Cam Valley	01/10/1918	03/10/1918
War Diary	Habarcq	04/10/1918	04/10/1918
War Diary	Cagnicourt	05/10/1918	05/10/1918
War Diary	Bourlon	06/10/1918	10/10/1918
War Diary	Naves	11/10/1918	11/10/1918
War Diary	Iwuy	12/10/1918	19/10/1918
War Diary	Avesnes-Le-Sec	20/10/1918	20/10/1918
War Diary	Noyelles Sur-Selle	21/10/1918	24/10/1918
War Diary	Thiant	25/10/1918	31/10/1918
Heading	War Diary of 255th (Highland) Bde. R.F.A.T. for month of November, 1918. Vol 42		
War Diary	Maing	01/11/1918	03/11/1918
War Diary	Sebourquiax	06/11/1918	07/11/1918
War Diary	Angre	08/11/1918	08/11/1918
War Diary	Wiheries	09/11/1918	09/11/1918
War Diary	Quevy Le Petit	09/11/1918	09/11/1918
War Diary	Esquillies	10/11/1918	11/11/1918
War Diary	Givry	11/11/1918	27/11/1918
War Diary	Roeulx	28/11/1918	30/11/1918
Heading	War Diary of 255th Bde R.F.A.T. for month of December, 1918. Vol 43		
War Diary	Roeulx.	01/12/1918	31/12/1918
Heading	War Diary Of 255th Brigade R.F.A.T. for month of January 1919. Vol 44		

War Diary	Roeulx.	01/01/1919	31/01/1919
War Diary	Roeulx.	01/02/1919	28/02/1919
War Diary	Roeulx.	01/03/1919	31/03/1919

WO 95 2854/3

255 Brigade Royal Field Artillery
1915 June – 1919 March

51ST DIVISION

255TH (HIGHLAND) BDE RFA
JUN 1915 - MAR 1919

121/5930

a2
a/6

51st Division

1/1 Highland Field RTH

Vol I. 1 — 30.6.16.

Army Form C. 2118.

WAR DIARY
INTELLIGENCE SUMMARY.
(Erase heading not required.)

Place	Date	Hour	Summary of Events and Information	Remarks and references to Appendices
In the field	1915			
	1st June to 22nd June		Brigade in action —	
	23rd June		One battery withdrawn on 18th June owing to four guns ceasing to be effective —	
	24th June		Brigade withdrawn from action —	
	25th June		Brigade (2 batteries) went into action about two miles further north —	
	26th June to 30th June		Brigade (2 batteries) in action —	
	Present Date			

MacDuwall
LIEUT. COL. R.F.A. (T.)
COMMANDING 1/1st HIGHLAND F.A. BRIGADE.

51st Division

121/6437

1/1 Highland Bde RFA.

Vol II.

From 1st to 30th July 1915

Army Form C. 2118

WAR DIARY
or
INTELLIGENCE SUMMARY.
(Erase heading not required.)

1/1 Highland F.A. Brigade

Place	Date	Hour	Summary of Events and Information	Remarks and references to Appendices
In the Field	July 1 — 9th		Brigade in Action	
	" 10th — 19th		Brigade Resting	
	" 19th — 22nd		Brigade in Action	
	" 23rd — 26th		Brigade Resting	
	" 26th — 30th		Entraining & Detraining of Brigade.	

J. Williamson Capt. for
LIEUT. COL. R.F.A. (T.)
COMMANDING 1/1st HIGHLAND F.A. BRIGADE.

121/6598

51st Division

1/1 Highland Bde R.F.A.

Vol III

From 1 - 31. 8. 15

Army Form C. 2118.

WAR DIARY
or
INTELLIGENCE SUMMARY.
(Erase heading not required.)

1/1 High. F.A. Brigade

Instructions regarding War Diaries and Intelligence Summaries are contained in F. S. Regs., Part II. and the Staff Manual respectively. Title pages will be prepared in manuscript.

Place	Date	Hour	Summary of Events and Information	Remarks and references to Appendices
In the field	1/5/15	—	Bde Commander with Bty Comdrs reconnoitred new front with French Artillery	
"	3/5/15	—	Batteries relieved 35th Regiment of Artillery 1st Groupe French Artillery & took over their positions & zones.	
"	2/5/15	—	Brigade received new 18 pr. Guns & equipment from Base.	
"	2/5/15	—	Brigade fired with new guns, registering their zones, & returned 15 pr Guns & equipment out of action.	
"	3/5/15	—	Bde Head Quarters received a Wireless Installation from Flying Corps for use between Batteries & Flying Machines.	

W.W. Duncan
LIEUT. COL. R.F.A. (T.)
COMMANDING 1/1st HIGHLAND F.A. BRIGADE.

121/7051

51st Division

1/1 Highland Bde R.F.A.

Vol IV

Sept. 15.

WAR DIARY
or
INTELLIGENCE SUMMARY.
(Erase heading not required.)

Army Form C. 2118.

Place	Date	Hour	Summary of Events and Information	Remarks and references to Appendices
In the Field 1915	23/9/15		Brigade still in action	
"			1st Battery — Wire-cutting at 424 & behind 424 M.G's	
			2nd C of A Battery — Wire-cutting at 434 & behind 433 M.G's	
			3rd C of A Battery — Wire-cutting at 412 & 417	
"	24/9/15		1st C of A Battery — Wire cutting — 100 yds N. of 424 & behind M.G. at 423	
			2nd C of A Battery — Wire cutting — 200 yds N of 433, M.G. 100 yds N of 434 & M.G. 150 yds S of 434	
			3rd C of A Battery — Wire cutting — 467 each of 408 & 407, M.G. East of 415	
"	25/9/15		1st C of A Battery — Wire cutting — 431	
			2nd C of A Battery — Wire cutting — 170x N of 433, 2 M.G's 90 yds N. of 431	
			3rd C of A Battery — Wire cutting — 408	
"	25—30		Brigade still in action.	

Williamson Lt for
LIEUT. COL. R.F.A.(T.)
COMMANDING 1/1st HIGHLAND F.A. BRIGADE.

D/7449

51st Division

1/1 Highland R.F.A. Bde.

Dec -15

—

Vol II

WAR DIARY or INTELLIGENCE SUMMARY

Army Form C. 2118

Place	Date	Hour	Summary of Events and Information	Remarks and references to Appendices
In the Field	1/Oct/1915	—	Location of Units at month of Oct. 1915. (Only change of position during month is 3rd C/of A. Battery as shown below) Position as follows:- Headqrs in ALBERT 1st C/of A Battery W.18.c.0.4 — Wagon Line BRESLE 2nd " " W.23.D.5.4 — do. 3rd " " W.3.B.3.0 — do. Amm Column — Wagon Line BAZIEUX.	
	2		Brigade in action all month covering F. sector, 154th Infy Bde (LA BOISSELLE to THIEPVAL shoulder) 2nd Renfrew Battery attached to Group on right 53rd Bde, 18th Division with 83rd F.A. Brigade covering them — also A 57H on left 152nd & 153rd Bdes alternately covered by 2nd H.F.A.Bde & D.83 H Battery	
	15th Oct.	3	3rd C of A Battery moved from X/18.A.12 to XX 3.D.3.0 near MARTINSART — French map 57.D. S.E. 4 1/10.000	
	25 Oct.	4	O.C. & 2 Majors attended inspection by H.M. the King near RIBEMONT.	

M.M.Duncan
LIEUT. COL. R.F.A. (T.)
COMMANDING 1/1st HIGHLAND F.A. BRIGADE.

51st Burears

1/ Highlands Bde R.F.A.
Nov. 1915
vol VI

121/
74/8

WAR DIARY
or
INTELLIGENCE SUMMARY.
(Erase heading not required.)

Army Form C. 2118.

Instructions regarding War Diaries and Intelligence Summaries are contained in F. S. Regs., Part II. and the Staff Manual respectively. Title pages will be prepared in manuscript.

Place	Date	Hour	Summary of Events and Information	Remarks and references to Appendices
Field	1/11/15		Brigade still in action	
"	8/11/15		1st C of A Battery, cut wire with gun in advanced position	
"	25/11/15		2nd " " cut wire with gun in advanced position	
"	29/11/15		1/1st C. of Edinburgh Battery — Relief of 1st C of A Battery commenced.	
"	30/11/15		2½ Batteries in action, one section, 1st C of A Battery resting	

WDuncan
LIEUT. COL. R.F.A. (T.)
COMMANDING 1/1st HIGHLAND F.A. BRIGADE.

51st Div

1/1 Highland Bde. R.F.A.
Dec 1915
Vol. VII

12/7957

Army Form C. 2118.

WAR DIARY
or
INTELLIGENCE SUMMARY.
(Erase heading not required.)

Instructions regarding War Diaries and Intelligence Summaries are contained in F. S. Regs., Part II. and the Staff Manual respectively. Title pages will be prepared in manuscript.

Place	Date	Hour	Summary of Events and Information	Remarks and references to Appendices
Field	1/12/15		2½ Batteries in action (½ 1st Aberdeen resting at BRESLE)	
"	2/12/15		Remaining Section 1st Aberdeen relieved by 1st Edinburgh & withdrew to BRESLE	
"	7/12/15		2nd Coy Edinburgh Battery came into Group	
"	18/12/15		3 Sections from Cheshire F.A. Brigade relieved Sections of 2nd & 3rd Aberdeen & 1st Edinburgh.	
"	20/12/15		Brigade Headqrs relieved by 1st Lowland F.A. Brigade HdQrs & withdrew to WARLOY	
"	24/12/15		Cheshire F.A. Brigade Sections withdrawn Brigade HdQrs resting at WARLOY	
"	31/12/15		1st Battery resting at BRESLE 2nd & 3rd Coy A. Batteries in action. Ammn Column at BAZIEUX	

Wwwdwwau Lt.Col.RFA(T)
Commdg 1/1 HFA Bde

New High? Bse R.E.A.
Jan 1946
vol VIII

Army Form C. 2118.

WAR DIARY
OF
INTELLIGENCE SUMMARY.
(Erase heading not required.)

Instructions regarding War Diaries and Intelligence Summaries are contained in F. S. Regs., Part II. and the Staff Manual respectively. Title pages will be prepared in manuscript.

Place	Date	Hour	Summary of Events and Information	Remarks and references to Appendices
Sully	1916 Jany 5		Head Quarters, 1st Batty & Am. Col. were moved to Rest Billets	
"	6		One section each of 2nd & 3rd Batteries relieved by sections 161st F.A. Bde. & withdrew to Wagon Lines	
"	7		Remaining sections 2nd & 3rd Btys relieved & withdrew to Wagon Lines, leaving B.C.'s & subaltern N.C.O.'s & signallers in gun positions 2nd & 3rd Batteries marched to rest Billets	
"	18		B.C.'s of 2nd & 3rd Batteries handed over gun positions etc. to 161 Brigade & withdrew with Subaltern, N.C.O's & signallers to rest billets.	
"	31		Brigade in Rest Billets.	

31/1/76.

J Williamsworth /pLt Col R.F.A (?)
Commdg 1st A.F.A Bde

WAR DIARY or INTELLIGENCE SUMMARY.

(Erase heading not required.)

Army Form C. 2118.

Place	Date	Hour	Summary of Events and Information	Remarks and references to Appendices
ST Sauveur	Feby 1916 1/2/16		Brigade at rest — training	
Bussy les Daours	7		Brigade marched to BUSSY les DAOURS	
"	8		Brigade at rest — training	
"	15/16		C.O. at BRAY inspecting positions	
"	20		C.O. and 3 Majors moved to BRAY	
BRAY	22		One section 2nd Aberdeen relieved one section B/150 Brigade in action near SUZANNE (Centre group of Right Division.) One Section 1st Aberdeen relieved section from 2nd Aberdeen & ditto of C/150 & A/150	
	24		O/C 1/150 Batteries took over line. C.O. took over Group (3 Aberdeen Batteries 18 pdr. and 1st Renfrew 4.5 How.) relieving 150th F.A. Brigade. 2nd & 3rd Battery Wagon Lines in BRAY, shelled at 8 pm. 3 men killed, 4 wounded and 7 horses killed.	
	26		During heavy bombardment of MARICOURT wood in evening Lieut. L. Jenkins 1st Battery repaired 28 breaks in his line from Infy. Headqrs to Brigade Exchange.	
	27			

WAR DIARY
INTELLIGENCE SUMMARY.
(Erase heading not required.)

Army Form C. 2118.

Place	Date	Hour	Summary of Events and Information	Remarks and references to Appendices
BRAY	Feby 28		Brigade came out of action 150th F.A Brigade again taking over. Brigade marched to BUSSY les DAOURS	
VILLERS-BOCAGE	29		51st Divl Arty marched to VILLERS BOCAGE from BUSSY les DAOURS. Brigade now part of 17th Corps 4th Army.	

WWMaxwell
Lt Col RHA(T)
Commdg 1/I Highld F A Brigade

255 Bde RFA Vol 10 51

WAR DIARY
or
INTELLIGENCE SUMMARY.

Place	Date	Hour	Summary of Events and Information	Remarks and references to Appendices
Field	1916 March 1st		Brigade rested at VILLERS BOCAGE	
	6		Brigade marched to OCCOCHES	
	9			
	11		Brigade marched to BERLINCOURT	
	12		One section of each Battery in Brigade moved into action at FOND de VASE to relieve 34 Group French Artillery	
	30		Remaining sections of Brigade moved to FOND de VASE. C. & D/255 heavily shelled with 8.2"s, 3 men of D/255 killed, our wagon limber of C.255 completely destroyed by direct hit. In all 107 rounds 8.2" fired by Hun.	
	31		A very successful shoot carried out in connection with our of our mines at 7 p.m.	

Williamson Lt for
Lieut Col RFA T
Commdg 255th Hy. Brigade RFA T

WAR DIARY
INTELLIGENCE SUMMARY.
(Erase heading not required.)

Army Form C. 2118.

Place	Date	Hour	Summary of Events and Information	Remarks and references to Appendices
FOND DE VASE	1916 April 1		Brigade in action. (Battery Wagon lines and B.A.C. at FREVIN CAPELLE).	
near MAROEUIL	" "	April 6th	12th Renforcs in front.	
	" 8		Personnel for additional Battery arrived railhead.	
			Several additional officers joined. 36 officers now in Brigade.	
	" 11th		D Battery formed at 12 noon. Officers in Brigade rearranged.	
	" 16		Guns' position and especially 2nd Aberdeen shelled. (81. from 21 cm. mortar). One gun knocked out	
	" "	11.45 pm	2 Lieut. W. Robertson buried in dug out at 10 pm, heard him speak 5 hrs. got him out none the worse at 1.45 pm. Lieut. C.H. Millar, Sergt. Lebingham W., Bomb. Flatt W., Bombr. Hardie J. & Gr. Allen (Lt. Millar, Sgt. Lebingham, and Gr. Allen wounded) recommended for gallantry in digging under fire. (Major Garden also slightly wounded.	
	" 23		D. 110 joined Group relieving C.112.	
	" 25		Divisional Artillery shoot on trenches opposite N.1.	
	" 27		N. sector heavily bombarded. - Batteries retaliated all forenoon.	
	" 28		5 mines exploded on left of M. Sector at 2.15 am. S.O.S. from N.1. Huns tried to leave his trenches but failed. Matters quietened down after an hour or so.	
	" 29	9.30 am	Hun aeroplane brought down in near of front position.	

WAR DIARY
or
INTELLIGENCE SUMMARY.

Army Form C. 2118.

Place	Date	Hour	Summary of Events and Information	Remarks and references to Appendices
FOND DE VASE near MAROEUIL	1916 April 30		Group (1st, 2nd, & 3rd Aberdeen, 1st Renfrew (How"), and D.110) in action at FOND de VASE. D Battery (personnel only) Battery Wagon lines + B.A.C. at FREVIN CAPELLE.	
	"			
	"			

WM Duncan
Lieut. Col. R.F.A.,
Commanding 1/1 Highland F. A. Brigade.

WAR DIARY or INTELLIGENCE SUMMARY

Army Form C. 2118.

255th (HIGHLAND) BRIGADE, R.F.A. (T.)
No. 230
Date 31/5/16

late H/y
High B.M.

Place	Date	Hour	Summary of Events and Information	Remarks and references to Appendices
Field Fond de Vase near Maroeuil	1916 May 1st		Group (1st, 2nd & 3rd Aberdeen, 1st Renfrew (How) & D/110 in action at Fond de Vase. D Battery (personnel only), Battery Wagon Lines & B.A.C at Frevin-Capelle.	
	15		Orders received as to re-arrangement of Artillery Brigades. 1/1 High. F.A. Brigade became 255th (Highland) Brigade and consists of 1st City of Aberdeen Battery called A.255 2nd do do do called B.255 3rd do do do called C.255 1st Renfrew (How). called D.255 The new Battery D. Battery is transferred to 258th Brigade and called A.258 The B.A.C becomes No 1 Section, A. Echelon D.A.C.	
	18	12.30am	Mine exploded at A.10.A.95.80 (Roclincourt Sheet 51.B.N.W.1, Sq.2. 13 1/10.000) - commenced shoot & small raid - much damage done to trenches & many Germans reported killed. No prisoners taken - our casualties very slight.	
	19		Relief of 25th Div. Artillery by Centre Group 51st Divisional began.	
	21	3.30pm	Further relief of 23rd Div Artillery stopped. Heavy bombardment to the North about Q Sector began.	

Army Form C. 2118.

WAR DIARY
or
INTELLIGENCE SUMMARY.
(Erase heading not required.)

(2)

Instructions regarding War Diaries and Intelligence Summaries are contained in F. S. Regs., Part II. and the Staff Manual respectively. Title pages will be prepared in manuscript.

Place	Date	Hour	Summary of Events and Information	Remarks and references to Appendices
FOND DE VASE near MAROEUIL	1916 May 21st		Tear shells at BETHUNE O.P. and some of the Battery positions	
	22	4 pm	Heavy bombardment on the North	
	25	8.15 pm	Artillery shoot on front line opposite M2 & N1	
	26		Orders received to bring back Batteries from 25th Div. Area - Artillery regrouped Left Group formed of 255 and 257 Brigades under Lt. Col. Duncan.	
	28		Orders received that taking over 25th Divl. Arty. positions as proposed on 19th should not be carried out.	
	29/30		Relief of 25th Divl. Artillery by 257 Brigade carried out	
	30/31		New Centre Group consisting of 255 Brigade, A/258 & D/257 under Lt. Col. Duncan formed.	
	31		A.B.C.D. 255 in action at FOND DE VASE - Wagon line at FREVIN-CAPELLE	

31/5/16

WW Duncan Lieut. Col. RFA (I)
Commdg. 255th (High.) Brigade RFA (T.F.)

WAR DIARY
or
INTELLIGENCE SUMMARY.
(Erase heading not required.)

Army Form C. 2118.

255 Bde R.F.A.

Place	Date	Hour	Summary of Events and Information	Remarks and references to Appendices
FOND DE VASE	June 1st		Centre Group consisting of (A, B, C, D.255, A/258, D.260) in action in FOND de VASE. Wagon Lines at FREVIN CAPELLE	
	2nd		A/111 Battery joined Centre Group. B/111 do do	
	3rd	8.48pm	Artillery Scheme No. 7, Raid, 3 mines fired. Batteries firing for 1 hour 20 minutes, thanked by G.O.C. 51st Division for accurate fire	
	16th		A/122 and B/119 relieved A & B/111	
	25th		4 Days bombardment of trenches in front of Right Group began.	
	27th		B.300 & B.303 relieved A.122 & B.119	
	28th		Attempted Raid by Enemy in O Sector (B.255's Zone). Enemy caught by our fire when retiring. Enemy Raid on M.2 Sector (A.258's Zone) at 3 a.m. Infantry suffered casualties.	
	30th		D.260 (How) withdrew from Group. 2 Colonels R.A. 60th Division arrived. Centre Group (A.B.C. D/255, A/258, B.300 & B.303) in action FOND de Vase — Wagon Lines still at FREVIN Capelle. Pro FONDEVAL.	

Wm Duncan
LIEUT. COL. R.F.A. (T.)
COMMANDING ~~THE~~ HIGHLAND F.A. BRIGADE.
255

CONFIDENTIAL.
No 367/A
HIGHLAND
DIVISION.

Vol 14

Confidential

War Diary
of
253rd Brigade R.F.A.

From 1st July 1916 to 31st July 1916

(Volume)

WAR DIARY or INTELLIGENCE SUMMARY

Army Form C. 2118.

No 309 Y/A
HIGHLAND DIVISION

Place	Date	Hour	Summary of Events and Information	Remarks and references to Appendices
FOND de VASE	July 1		Centre Group (A.B.C. D/255, A/258, B.300 & B.303) in action FOND DE VASE, PROFONDVAL	
"	7		Wagon Lines at FREVIN CAPELLE	munshal
"	13		Raid from "PULPIT" on SHEBA'S BREASTS unsuccessful	munshal
"	14		Raid near oat MILL. 1 Prisoner taken - blown up.	munshal
"	15		Received orders at 4 p.m. to withdraw Brigade from action without to Wagon Lines	munshal
"	16		Marched from FREVIN Capelle to GROUCHES - 13 miles - started 6.30 a.m. arrived 1.30 p.m.	munshal
"	19		Marched from GROUCHES to HEM started 9.30 a.m. arrived 12 noon.	munshal
"	20		Marched 6.30 p.m. for HAVERNAS	munshal
"	21		Arrived HAVERNAS 2 a.m. Marched at 5.30 p.m. for DERNANCOURT	munshal
"	23		Arrived at DERNANCOURT 2.30 a.m. Motored FRICOURT. Inspected 94th Bde. Positions	munshal
"			Relieved 78th Brigade. A & B South of Bois de MAMETZ, C & B West of Bois de MAMETZ, D. South East of Bois de MAMETZ	munshal
"	24		Took over from 94th Brigade. High Wood	munshal
"	25		Attack by 154th Infantry Brigade on HIGH WOOD attacked at 8.15 p.m. Attack repulsed in evening failed	munshal

WAR DIARY
INTELLIGENCE SUMMARY.

Army Form C. 2118.

Place	Date	Hour	Summary of Events and Information	Remarks and references to Appendices
	July			
	30		Attack by 153rd Infantry Brigade on HIGH WOOD and WOOD LANE	unsuccessful
	31		Brigade still in action as above. Wagon lines near MEAULTE.	

M M Dulcan
Lieut. Col. R.F.A.
Commdg 255th (High) Brigade R.F.A.

51st Divisional Artillery.

255th BRIGADE

ROYAL FIELD ARTILLERY.

AUGUST 1 9 1 6

WAR DIARY
or
INTELLIGENCE SUMMARY.
(Erase heading not required.)

Army Form C. 2118.

CONFIDENTIAL
No. 21 (A)
NIGHT ONE

Place	Date	Hour	Summary of Events and Information	Remarks and references to Appendices
	1916 Aug. 1st		Brigade in action (3 Batteries making 2, 6 gun Batteries, 18 pdrs) near MAMETZ WOOD. Wagon lines near MEAULTE.	JW
	2		Bombardment of HIGH WOOD at 10 am & 4 p.m.	JW
	3		do. do. at 9.50 am.	JW
	5		B255 heavily shelled in afternoon	JW
	6		do. do. all day.	JW
	7		Bombardment of WOOD LANE TRENCH to assist Division on our right in evening	JW
	8		do. do. repeated in early morning. B255 heavily shelled all day about 3 pm, 8" guns concentrated on Battery, attachments fortunately cleared to flank — Major Garden, Lieut. R. W. Davidson (attached from C Battery) + Lieut. A. G. Macdonell buried. Former two slightly wounded. Position abandoned.	JW JW
	9		Met Lieut Col. 46 Bde, 14th Division and made arrangements about reinf. half of A + D Batteries relieved in evening.	JW
	10		Remainder of A + D Batteries relieved in evening — handed over to 46 Brigade at 7 pm. Headquarters marched to Wagon Line.	JW

WAR DIARY
or
INTELLIGENCE SUMMARY.
(Erase heading not required.)

Army Form C. 2118.

Place	Date	Hour	Summary of Events and Information	Remarks and references to Appendices
	Aug			
	11		Brigade marched to BONNAY	
	12		At BONNAY	
	13		In evening Battery marched to LONGUEAU & entrained.	
	14		Headquarters marched to SALEUX & entrained	
			Batteries arrived at STEENBECQUE	
			Hdqrs. arrived at ARQUES	
	16		Brigade marched to SERCUS. O.C. & B.C's motored to ARMENTIERES. One section of each Battery marched to ARMENTIERES to relieve 2nd F.A. Brigade N.Z. Division.	
	17		Remaining sections came into action. Relief complete in evening. Wagon lines at PONT de NIEPPE	
	21		Conference at C.R.A.'s arrangements made for Batteries being made into 6 gun Batteries by following additions:— Right Section A258 to A Battery, Right Section C258 to B " , Left Section A258 to C "	

Army Form C. 2118.

WAR DIARY
or
INTELLIGENCE SUMMARY. —3—
(Erase heading not required.)

Instructions regarding War Diaries and Intelligence Summaries are contained in F. S. Regs., Part II. and the Staff Manual respectively. Title pages will be prepared in manuscript.

Place	Date	Hour	Summary of Events and Information	Remarks and references to Appendices
	Aug 23		Right group formed at 12 noon consisting of A,B,C 255, A 256 all 18 pdr 6 gun Batteries, D255 & D256 4 gun How.d Batteries. Covering 154th Hy. Brigade.	Jn5
	25		152nd Hy. Bde relieved 154 Hy. Bde. 3 Battery Wagon Lines moved to new lines near JESUS Farm.	Jn5
	31		Raid by 153 Inf.y Brigade on left supported by certain Batteries of Group — unsuccessful. Group as above in action in front of ARMENTIERES.	Jn5.

J Williamson Lt/Col
Lieut Col R.F.A.T
Comm.g 255th Hy. Bde R.F.A.T

CONFIDENTIAL.
No 21/A.
HIGHLAND
DIVISION.

Vol 16

War Diary
of
255th (High) Brigade R.F.A.T

1st Sept 1916 to 30th Sept 1916

Copiedens?

Army Form C. 2118.

WAR DIARY
or
INTELLIGENCE SUMMARY.
(Erase heading not required.)

Instructions regarding War Diaries and Intelligence Summaries are contained in F. S. Regs., Part II. and the Staff Manual respectively. Title pages will be prepared in manuscript.

Place	Date	Hour	Summary of Events and Information	Remarks and references to Appendices
ARMENTIERES	1st		Group consisting of 255th Brigade + A + D/256. Brigade in action in front of Wagon Lines between town & STEENWERCK	
	4	6 am	Lion Col Dyson RFA 256th Brigade took over Group.	
			Gas attack by us & bombardment, no infantry action	
	5		Town shelled. One Brigade casualty.	
	12		Divl Horse Show :- Brigade won following prizes :- Best Lot: L.D. Horse 1st (A)	
			2nd (D) Best Turnout (Wagon + team) 1st (A) Driving (2 Wagon teams) 2nd (D) & 3rd (C)	
			Jumping N.C.O's 2nd (A) Best Heavy Weight Charger 1st (D) Officers Jumping 2nd (D)	
			(letter in brackets indicates Battery making entry).	
	14		Brigade Headquarters moved from Rue St Roch to G.O.C's House in RUE DENIS	Paper
	15	8·55 pm	Raid on Railway Junction Salients - former most successful - wire cut by torpedoes. 1 prisoner taken, about 50 Germans killed. Our casualties very slight. Group co-operated.	
	16	8·30 pm	Raid by 9th Royal Scots near L'EPINETTE, no prisoner taken but identification obtained, several casualties. Brigade co-operated.	
	19	11 am	CRA distributed Divisional Cards for Gallantry to Divisional Artillery. The following Officers + men in Brigade received cards :-	

WAR DIARY
or
INTELLIGENCE SUMMARY.
(Erase heading not required.)

Army Form C. 2118.

Place	Date	Hour	Summary of Events and Information	Remarks and references to Appendices
ARMENTIERES.			Lieut C. H. Millar Sgt. Flett B. Bty. Cpl. Clouston B/Bty. Cpl. Harold B/Bty.	wind
	23	12:30 am	Gunners Minihan Meagan & Driver Jim R. A/Bty.	
			Raid by 6th Gordons on Mushroom - unsuccessful owing to failure of Bangalore Torpedoes. Group Co-operated. One Section of B.C.D. 253 relieved by 34th Divisional Artillery (Col. Furnival's Brigade) and withdrawn to wagon lines.	wind
		8 pm	Remaining Sections of Group withdrawn and 255th Bde reached to CAUDESCURE	wind
CAUDESCURE	24	9 am	Command of Group handed over to Col Furnival. Bde. HdQrs. reached to CAUDESCURE via Sailly-Estaires	wind. Enemy Bergues
do.	25	5:30 am	Bde. marched to RAIMBERT via MERVILLE - ROBECQ - LILLERS - arrived 3 pm.	wind
RAIMBERT	26	7 am	Bde marched to BERGUENEUSE via PERNES - BOYAVAL - arrived 1 pm.	wind
BERGUENEUSE	27	7 am	Bde. marched to VACQUERIE LE BOUCQ via CROISETTE - CONCHY-SUR-CANCHE arrived 4 pm.	wind
VACQUERIE le BOUCQ	28	4:45 am	Bde. marched to BOIS du WARNIMONT via BONNIERES - BARLY - CHAT. OCCOCHES - DOULLENS - SARTON arrived 5:30 pm	wind
Bois du WARNIMONT	29	8:30 am	Brigade marched to PUSHVILLERS via AUTHIE - MARIEUX arrived 11:30 am.	wind
PUSHVILLERS	29	3 pm	CRA motored with Colonels to MARTINSART to inspect positions to be taken over from 44th Divl Artillery (Col. Stevenson)	wind
"	30	10 am	B.C.'s rode to MARTINSART	wind
		1 pm	One section from each Battery went into action near MARTINSART & MESNIL. Remainder of Brigade at PUSHVILLERS.	wind

Wm Duncan Lt. Col. R.F.A.T
Comdg. 255th (High) Bde. R.F.A.T

WAR DIARY
or
INTELLIGENCE SUMMARY

(Erase heading not required.)

Army Form C. 2118.

Place	Date 1916	Hour	Summary of Events and Information	Remarks and references to Appendices
MISNIL	Oct 1	12 m.n.	One section each Battery in action near MARTINSART MESNIL. Remainder of Brigade at PUCHVILLERS. Group consisted of 255 Brigade & C.85	hwd
"	"	10 am	Remaining sections moved into action. Wagon lines moved to VARENNES except C. to HEDAUVILLE	hwd
"	2nd	10 am	Head Qr moved into action	hwd
"	3rd		Remaining Battery Wagon lines moved to HEDAUVILLE. C/85 rejoined own Division	hwd
"	5		O/C. reconnoitred positions opposite PUSIEUX-au-MONTS.	hwd
"	6	9 am	Brigade with drew and marched to BUS-en-ARTOIS	hwd
COLINCAMPS	7	10 am	B. & C. Batteries moved 2 sections into action. Battery's made camouflage position. Headqn moved to COURCELLES. O/c in charge of composite Brigade — A/256. B & C/255 & D/256	hwd
do	10	10am	A 255 moved section into action. Remainder of Brigade Granville moved into action. a gun came back from I.O.M.	hwd
do	15	6 pm	Message received to stop work on position. Group broken up.	hwd
do	16	7.30pm	Raid by 4th Gordons and 6th Black Watch covered by fire of 255 & 256 Brigades. 4th Gordon got in but no prisoner	hwd
do	16	9 pm		hwd

WAR DIARY or INTELLIGENCE SUMMARY

Army Form C. 2118.

(Erase heading not required.)

Place	Date	Hour	Summary of Events and Information	Remarks and references to Appendices
MAILLY-MAILLET	16	9—	Batteries except A came out of action and went to Wagon Lines at BUS	hund
	17	10 am	OC reconnoitred positions between MAILLY-MAILLET & ENGELBELMER. Batteries came into action in evening. (Camouflage position)	hund
	18	10 am	Head Qrs moved up & relieved 179 Brigade. Wagon lines moved to VARENNES	hund
	19	10 am	OC reconnoitred position for 161 Brigade (the 2 Groups to consist of 161 & 255 Brigades) for attack on BEAUMONT-HAMEL	hund
	20	8 pm	161 Brigade came into action. 255 Batteries busy wire cutting	hund
	23		Z day postponed until 26th	hund
	24		Z day " " 28th.	hund
	26	5.30	Raid by 6th Black Watch & 7th Gordons covered by Group fire. 7th Gordons got prisoner. 6th Black Watch did not get in.	hund
	28		Z day postponed until 1st.	hund
	29		Lieutenm French Mortar 3rd Canadian Division put under Group for trenches.	hund
MAILLY-MAILLET	31	4 pm	Brigade in action between MAILLY-MAILLET & ENGELBELMER. Wagon Lines at VARENNES. Z day postponed to 5 Novr. 1916.	hund

WW Duncan
Lt Col R FA T
Comndg 255 Bde R FA T

CONFIDENTIAL.

WAR DIARY

of

255th (Highland) Brigade R.F.A.T.

for month of

October, 1916.

CONFIDENTIAL.
No
HIGHLAND
DIVISION.

SECRET.   For Liaison Officer   Copy No. _____

51st DIVISIONAL ARTILLERY.

OPERATION ORDER No. 58.

23rd October, 1916.

1. On the Z day the Reserve Army will attack and establish itself on the line MIRAUMONT – BEAUREGARD DOVECOTE – SERRE. The II Corps will attack south of the ANCRE and the V Corps north of the ANCRE.
    The V Corps will attack with 5 Divisions 63rd Division (on the right), 51st Division, 2nd Division, and 3rd Division (on the left) and the 37th Division.
    The frontage of the 51st Division is from Q.17a.8.8. to Q.5a.2½.0.
    The inner flanks of the attacks of the 2nd and 63rd Divisions will converge on Square R.1.central.
    The 51st Division will capture BEAUMONT HAMEL and will push forward between the converging flanks of the 2nd and 63rd Divisions as far as FRANKFORT TRENCH (running north and south through Q.6 central) between GLORY LANE and LEAVE AVENUE which it will consolidate.

2. The 51st Division will attack on the frontage of 2 Brigades, the 153rd Infantry Brigade on the right and the 152nd Infantry Brigade on the left.
    The 154th Infantry Brigade will be in reserve with Headquarters at CAMP JOURDAIN.
    The boundaries of the attack will be:-
    On the North a line running due west from Q.6 central.
    On the South a line running due west from Q.6d.5.4. to Q.6d.0.4. and thence in a south westerly direction to Q.17a.8.8.

3. The objectives of the 51st Division will be :-
    1st objective.) The line shewn in green on attached map
    2nd objective.   The line shewn in yellow on attached map

4. The attack will be prepared for an 'intense' bombardment for 48 hours previous to zero.

5. The arrangements for the Artillery barrage for the attack are shewn in Table A (Attached).
    The Brigade zones and barrage lines are shewn on attached map.
    Group Commanders will arrange for 25% of their 18 pounder guns to fire 50 yards short of the front line trench from zero to zero plus one minute.

6. Each Group Commander will arrange for his own lane using the batteries best suited for each part of lane.
    4.5's must search all communication trenches as near to our troops as is safe. The best enfilade possible being obtained. Remaining 4.5" Howrs. will always shoot on the barrage line beyond that on which the 18 pounders are shooting moving thus ahead of the 18 pounder barrage.
    O's.C. No.1 and No.4 Groups will detail one 18 pounder battery each to shoot in enfilade on selected areas, for times stated on attached Table B.
    On completion of programme these batteries will join their own group.
    Each Group will have one 18 pounder Battery used as a "thickening barrage" Battery so that it can be put on to another target without making a gap in the barrage.
    O.C. Groups will make Schemes for batteries as simple as they possibly can. It should be impressed on B.C's that fire must be aimed actually at the trench ordered and no safety allowance allowed in case of 18 pounder Batteries.
    Fuzes should be kept Graz/1 in 4 to be kept on graze. A safety allowance in range should be given for the 4.5" Hows.
    Battery Commanders are reminded that as most of the

/about.

barrage/-

CONFIDENTIAL

WAR DIARY.

Of

255th BRIGADE, ROYAL FIELD ARTILLERY.

From 1st November to 30th November 1916.

Army Form C. 2118.

WAR DIARY
or
INTELLIGENCE SUMMARY.
(Erase heading not required.)

Place	Date	Hour	Summary of Events and Information	Remarks and references to Appendices
	1916 Nov. 1st		Brigade in action between ENGLEBELMER and MAILLY-MAILLET - forming a Group with 161 Brigade R.F.A. (Colonel Bottom)	
	2nd		Z day to be 5th. Wagon lines West of VARENNES. Weather very wet. Trenches almost impassable.	mund
	3rd		Z day to be 7th.	mund
	4th		Z day postponed indefinitely on account of weather.	mund
	5th	4.30 4.35pm	Bombardment by Artillery - heavy reply by enemy. Several casualties among Infantry.	mund
		8.50 8.55am	Bombardment by Artillery.	mund
	6th	1.10 1.15	Z day to be 9th (cancelled in evening). Bombardment by Artillery.	mund
	10th		Z day to be 13th.	mund
	11th		All Batteries fired 200 rounds a gun wire cutting.	mund
	12th		All Batteries fired 150 rounds a gun wire cutting. Lieut. Col. Duncan left for liaison with 153 Infantry Brigade. 2Lt. (temp. Lieut.) M'Lean left for liaison with 6th Black Watch. Col. Bottom took over command of Group. Weather the last few days dirier.	mund
	13th	5.45am	Barrage commenced in accordance with 51st D.A. O.O. no. 58(?) No. 59(2) & amendments B.M. 304/34(3)	App. 1, 2 r 3

Army Form C. 2118.

WAR DIARY
or
INTELLIGENCE SUMMARY.
(Erase heading not required.)

Instructions regarding War Diaries and Intelligence Summaries are contained in F. S. Regs., Part II. and the Staff Manual respectively. Title pages will be prepared in manuscript.

Place	Date	Hour	Summary of Events and Information	Remarks and references to Appendices
	1916 Nov.			
	13th	5.45am	B.M.304/28(4). B.M.304/38(5). Very thick morning. Everything invisible at 50 yards but taken about	App 4.15
		9.33am	100 to 150 yards could be seen. Barrage in accordance with above completed.	
		10 am.	Slow Barrage continued beyond Yellow Line (FRANKFORT Trench). 6th Black Watch who advanced under cover of Brigade Barrage reported it excellent. Few casualties in taking enemy front line. Wire reported no obstacle.	
		4.30pm	Barrage ceased.	
		5.30pm	Message received that enemy massing to attack FRANKFORT Trench. Barrage placed beyond Green line (slightly East of STATION ROAD).	
		6.30pm	Barrage ceased.	
		5.20pm	Night firing by 255 Brigade to be in FRANKFORT Trench.	
		6.15pm	Night firing changes to I line (about 400 yards East of STATION Road). During the day the Highland Division took BEAUMONT HAMEL and Y Ravine and during night were consolidating East of STATION Road. About 1000 prisoners taken.	MuD
	14th	5.50am	Barrage on zones as ordered by 51st D.A.O.O. No. 60 (b) commenced.	App 6
		12.30 pm	Barrage ceased.	

WAR DIARY
or
INTELLIGENCE SUMMARY.
(Erase heading not required.)

Army Form C. 2118.

Instructions regarding War Diaries and Intelligence Summaries are contained in F. S. Regs., Part II. and the Staff Manual respectively. Title pages will be prepared in manuscript.

Place	Date	Hour	Summary of Events and Information	Remarks and references to Appendices
	1916 Nov.			
	14th	2.45 p.m.	Barrage on FRANKFORT Trench.	
		2.51 p.m.	Barrage ceased.	
		11.30 p.m.	Night firing by 255 Bde. on FRANKFORT Trench. Searching most distant approaches in accordance with B.M. 563 (5). The mist was not so thick on this day.	wind app 7.
	15th	5.45 a.m.	Barrage by A/255 - 50 yards beyond FRANKFORT Trench between GLORY Lane and LEAVE Avenue as signed of 63rd D.A. who reported counter attack expected.	App 8
		6.20 a.m.	Barrage ceased.	
		9 a.m.	Night firing by 161 Bde. Barrage turned on MUNICH trench &c. in accordance with B.M. 564 (8).	App 9
		4 p.m.	Barrage ceased.	App 10
		11 p.m.	Night firing by 161 Bde. on most distant roads and approaches in accordance with B.M. 304/4 (9) amended by B.M. 566 (10). Bursts of fire by 255 Bde. during night on S.O.S. line beyond FRANKFORT trench in accordance with B.M. 304/41. Lt. Col. Duncan returned from Liaison and resumed command of Group. 2/Lt. (Temp. Lt.) Millar returned from Liaison. 152 + 153 Infantry Brigades relieved by 154 Inf. Bde.	App 11.
	16th	9 p.m.	Night firing by 161 Bde. as on previous night in accordance with B.M. 566 (4). Bursts of fire by 255 Bde. as on previous night in accordance with B.M. 566. Attached No. 123 is map showing the condition of the wire as has inspected on this date.	App 12

WAR DIARY
or
INTELLIGENCE SUMMARY.
(Erase heading not required.)

Army Form C. 2118.

Place	Date	Hour	Summary of Events and Information	Remarks and references to Appendices
	1916 Nov. 16th		Note:- Map does not show any wire between O.11.c.5.6. and O.10.d.9.8.9.a. The wire in front of this trench was very thick when wire cutting operations commenced and was completely removed.	
			Attached (No.13) is map showing British front line on this date.	App 13
			Attached (No.14) is barrage fire for 13th for No.1 Gun of 6/255	App 14
			Attached (No.15) is note of Ammunition fired by Group 13th/14th November.	App 15
			Ammunition fired by 255 Bde. from 19th October to 14th Nov. was 4.7, 4.62. 18 Pounders. 4.152. 4.5 Howitzers. On this date 161 Brigade left Group.	WWW
	19th	12.30pm	3 mats of fire on MUNICH & FRANKFORT Trenches, LEAVE Avenue, and RYCROFT Alley.	WWW
		2.30pm	Barrage on same trenches supporting attack by Division on our right.	WWW
	23rd		Batteries withdrew from action to Wagon Lines.	WWW
	24th		One Section per Battery moved into action near COURCELETTE taking over from 1st Canadian Division. Wagon Lines moved to Brickfield area near ALBERT.	WWW
	25th		Headquarters & remainder of Batteries moved into action. H.qrs. in SUCRERIE. Very wet day.	WWW
	27th		H.qrs. moved to Hedges. of 70th Canadian Bde. between POZIERES & OVILLERS.	WWW
	29th		Brigade with A.B. & D./260 formed into Right Group under Lieut. Col. M.M. Duncan evening 2 Battalions 153 Brigade.	WWW

Army Form C. 2118.

WAR DIARY
or
INTELLIGENCE SUMMARY.
(Erase heading not required.)

Instructions regarding War Diaries and Intelligence Summaries are contained in F. S. Regs., Part II. and the Staff Manual respectively. Title pages will be prepared in manuscript.

Place	Date	Hour	Summary of Events and Information	Remarks and references to Appendices
Brigade in action near COURCELETTE.	1916 Nov 30th		Wagon lines in Brickfield area near ALBERT.	*init*

W M Duncan
Lieut. Col. R.F.A.
Commanding 255th (Highland) Bde. R.F.A.

Secret.

War Diary
of
255th (Highland) Brigade R.F.A.T.
for the month of
December, 1916.

CONFIDENTIAL. Army Form C. 2118.

No. 21(A)
HIGHLAND DIVISION.

WAR DIARY
or
INTELLIGENCE SUMMARY.
(Erase heading not required.)

Instructions regarding War Diaries and Intelligence Summaries are contained in F. S. Regs., Part II. and the Staff Manual respectively. Title pages will be prepared in manuscript.

Place	Date	Hour	Summary of Events and Information	Remarks and references to Appendices
COURCELETTE	1916 Dec. 1st	—	Brigade in action forming with 260th Brigade Right Group under O.C. 255th Brigade R.F.A.	Wyffel
		—	Wagon lines EAST & NORTH of ALBERT.	Wyffel
	6th	—	Command of Group handed over to O.C. 260th Brigade R.F.A.	Wyffel
	"	—	Lieut. Col. Duncan acting C.R.A. during General Oldfield's leave.	Wyffel
	17th	—	C.R.A. returned from leave. Lieut. Col. Duncan rejoined 255th Brigade.	Wyffel
	31st	—	Brigade in action forming with 260th Brigade Right Group under O.C. 260 Bde. R.F.A.	Wyffel
		—	Wagon lines EAST and NORTH of ALBERT.	Wyffel

H. Lawson Lieut. R.F.A.
for Lieut. Col. R.F.A.
Commanding 255th (Highland) Brigade R.F.A.

SECRET.

CONFIDENTIAL
No 2/(1)
HIGHLAND
DIVISION.

WAR DIARY

— OF —

255th (HIGHLAND) BRIGADE R.F.A.T.

— for the month of —

January, 1917.

Army Form C. 2118.

WAR DIARY
or
INTELLIGENCE SUMMARY.
(Erase heading not required.)

CONFIDENTIAL
No 21(A)
HIGHLAND DIVISION.

Place	Date	Hour	Summary of Events and Information	Remarks and references to Appendices
	1917			
COURCELETTE	Jan 3rd		Brigade in action forming with 260th Brigade Right Group under Lieut. Col. Oldham. R.F.A.	Nil
	4th		Wagon Lines East and North of ALBERT.	Nil
	5th		Commencement of relief by 36th Brigade R.F.A. Relief complete - Batteries withdrew to Wagon Lines.	Nil
SARTON	6th	9 am.	Brigade marched to SARTON.	Nil
GEZAINCOURT.	7th	9 am.	Brigade marched to GEZAINCOURT.	Nil
BEAUVOIR RIVIER	8th	9 am.	Brigade marched to BEAUVOIR RIVIERE.	Nil
GRAND LAVIERS	9th	6.30 am	Brigade marched to GRAND LAVIERS.	Nil
LAVIERS	10th/31st		Brigade training at GRAND LAVIERS.	Jas. Ct.

W. W. Duncan
Lieut. Col. R.F.A.Y.
Commanding 255th (Highland) Brigade R.F.A.Y.

SECRET.

Vol 21

War Diary
—of—
255th Brigade R.F.A.T.
—for month of—
February 1917.

WAR DIARY
or
INTELLIGENCE SUMMARY.

(Erase heading not required.)

Army Form C. 2118.

Place	Date 1917	Hour	Summary of Events and Information	Remarks and references to Appendices
GRAND LAVIERS	Feby 1-4th		Brigade resting and refitting.	
	5th	8:30 am	Marched from GRAND LAVIERS.	
		2:45 pm	Arrived at NOYELLE-en-CHAUSSEE (13½ miles)	
	6th	9 am	Marched from NOYELLE-en-CHAUSSEE.	
		12:20 pm	Arrived at CONCHY (13 miles)	
	7th	8:30 am	Marched from CONCHY.	
		12 noon	Arrived at CROIX (9 miles)	
	8th	9:30 am	Marched from CROIX.	
		1 pm	Arrived at MAGNICOURT-en-CONTÉ.	
MAGNICOURT	9th-18th		Brigade refitting.	
	10th		45 men sent forward to dig positions for Y.M.C.A.	
	12th		do. do. do.	
	16th		1 Officer & 45 men	
			O.C. went up to MADAGASCAR to inspect proposed gun positions.	
			First day of pronounced thaw.	
	19th	10:30 am	Marched from MAGNICOURT.	
		12 noon	Arrived at OURTON (4½ miles)	
OURTON	19th to 28th		Brigade refitting.	

J Williamson Hylr
Lieut. Col. R.F.A.
Commanding 255th Bde R.F.A.

Secret.

Vol 22

War Diary
of
255th (High.) Brigade R.F.A.
for month of
March 1917.

WAR DIARY
or
INTELLIGENCE SUMMARY.
(Erase heading not required.)

Army Form C. 2118.

Place	Date	Hour	Summary of Events and Information	Remarks and references to Appendices
OURTON	1919 March 1st		Brigade refitting.	unslttd
	9th		Brigade marched to FREVIN CAPELLE.	unslttd
	10th		Headquarters moved to near MADAGASCAR.	unslttd
	13th		Brigade took over Right half of Divisional zone in front of ROCLINCOURT.	unslttd
	17th		Raid by 1/8th Argyll & Sutherland Highlanders opposite ROCLINCOURT. (10 prisoners) Barrage reported very good.	unslttd
	31st		Raid by 1/6th Black Watch. No prisoners taken but identification got. Major G. Davidson A/255 wounded just prior to raid.	unslttd
MADAGASCAR			Brigade in action near MADAGASCAR Corner. Brigade Wagon Lines at FREVIN CAPELLE.	unslttd

W.W. Duncan
Lieut. Col. R.F.A.
Commanding 255th (High) Bde. R.F.A.

Secret.

War Diary
— of —
255th Brigade R.F.A.T.
— for month of —
April 1917.

WAR DIARY
or
INTELLIGENCE SUMMARY.
(Erase heading not required.)

Army Form C. 2118.

Instructions regarding War Diaries and Intelligence Summaries are contained in F.S. Regs., Part II. and the Staff Manual respectively. Title pages will be prepared in manuscript.

Place	Date 1917	Hour	Summary of Events and Information	Remarks and references to Appendices
MADAGASCAR	April 1/4th		Brigade in action near MADAGASCAR Corner. Wagon Lines at FREVIN CAPELLE. G.O. in command of No. 1 Group consisting of 34th A.F.A. Bde. 64th A.F.A. Bde. and 255th Bde. R.F.A.	
	3rd		Headquarters moved to MADAGASCAR Corner.	
	"		C Battery moved forward to ROCLINCOURT.	
	4/5th			
	9th	Z day.	Attack commenced (for orders see attached Papers "A").	
		5.30 am.		
		8 am.	Infantry reported to be advancing from BLACK Line.	
		12 noon	BLUE line reported taken.	
		12.15 pm	Limbers ordered to ANZIN.	
		2.40 pm.	F.O.O. (Lieut. J.J. White) ordered forward.	
		4 pm.	A., B. & D Batteries ordered forward to ROCLINCOURT.	
		4 pm.	A & B in action at ROCLINCOURT.	
	10th	12.30 am.	F.O.O. reports Infantry not in BROWN Line.	
		5 am.	Attack on BROWN Line on Gavrelle front unsuccessful.	
		7.45 am.	D Battery in action at ROCLINCOURT. Wagon line now E. of ANZIN.	
	11th	4 pm.	After BROWN line bombarded by H.A., reported unoccupied and occupied by our Infantry.	
			Division Infantry relieved during night.	
	11/12th		C.O. reconnoitred positions in 34th Division area on ARRAS- BAILLEUL Road. Orders afterwards cancelled.	
	12th		C.O. & B.Cs reconnoitred positions in 4th Division E. of ARRAS. Batteries & Headquarters came into action in afternoon.	
	13th		Orders received to exchange positions with 52nd A.F.A. Bde. Headqrs. in Railway Embankment.	
PONT DU JOUR	14th		Batteries moved into positions in Valley N. of ATHIES. Heavily shelled during night.	
	15th		Headqrs. moved to Zouave Trench.	
	14th		A., C. & D Batteries moved to new positions.	

WAR DIARY
INTELLIGENCE SUMMARY.
(Erase heading not required.)

Army Form C. 2118.

Place	Date 1917	Hour	Summary of Events and Information	Remarks and references to Appendices
PONT DU JOUR	April 18th		No. 1 Group formed (covering Right Bde. - 154th Inf. Bde.) of 23rd A.F.A. Bde., 51st Bde. & 255th Bde. R.F.A.	
	19th	3 am	Wagon lines moved to OIL FACTORY near ST NICHOLAS (8 hours in journey)	
		10 pm	do moved back to ANZIN wagon lines.	
	21st		Several casualties in brigade. Bombr. Cheyne & Bombr. McBain killed.	
	22nd		do Cpl. Thomson A/B. Main. G. Walker killed.	
			O.C. at liaison with 154th Infantry Bde.	
	23rd	4.45am	General attack. - 154th Brigade attacked Chemical Works & ROEUX under barrage fire.	
			Chemical Works taken and ROEUX occupied.	
		7.30 pm	Infantry driven out of Chemical Works & trench beyond also retired from ROEUX.	
		11.30 pm	Machine guns captured in Chemical Works. Infantry now holding enemy front line in CEYLON trench with switch dug south to River Scarpe.	
			Three counter attacks in afternoon broken by our fire. Lieut. Croil wounded & signaller killed	
	24th	4.30 am	Heavy counter attack from Chemical Works stopped by artillery and M.G. fire.	
			Batteries shelled with gas shell during night.	
	24/25th		O.C. returned from liaison with 154th Inf. Bde. 51st Division less artillery relieved by 34th Division.	
	25th	12 noon	34th D.A. relieved 51st D.A.	
	26th		Rest billet for 4 officers & 60 men arranged in ARRAS.	
	28th	4.25 am	General attack by 34th Division with 12th Division on right and 37th on left.	
			Brigade covering 101st Brigade with barrage fire.	
			ROEUX entirely cemetery occupied - no advance on Chemical Works.	
	29th	4 pm	Infantry back in line from which they started in morning - casualties heavy.	
	30th	3 am	Attempt by no. 2 to occupy Chemical Works without artillery support shelling with heavy loss.	
			Bde. at action N. of ATHIES.	
			Wagon lines at ANZIN.	

for Lt. Col. Comdg 255th Bde. R.F.A.

Secret.

War Diary
— of —
255th (High.) Bde. R.F.A.
— for month of —
May 1917

Vol 24

Army Form C. 2118.

WAR DIARY
or
INTELLIGENCE SUMMARY.
(Erase heading not required.)

Instructions regarding War Diaries and Intelligence Summaries are contained in F. S. Regs., Part II. and the Staff Manual respectively. Title pages will be prepared in manuscript.

Place	Date 1917 May	Hour	Summary of Events and Information	Remarks and references to Appendices
POINT DU JOUR	1st	3 am	Batteries in action N. of ATHIES. Wagon Lines at ANZIN.	For orders see App. A.
	2nd	7 pm	CHINESE barrage.	
			CHINESE barrage testing flanks.	
	3rd	3.30 pm	Barrage on enemy front line to enable Infantry to reoccupy their own front line.	For orders & barrage map see App. B.
		3.45 am	General attack by 1st, 3rd & 5th Armies. Brigade supporting 10th Inf. Bde. of 4th Division.	
		6.45 am	Barrage withdrawn to line 114 on left to line 4 on right.	
		7.45 am	Barrage on line 114 for whole Brigade.	
		9.10 am	New barrage line I.20.b.0.9. I.20.b.0.3. I.20.c.0.9.	
		9.45 am	9th Division on left back in their own front line. 4th Division hold part of Chemical Works but back in front line on right.	
		1 pm	About 300 men, hostile prisoners, seen going East from ROEUX.	
		2.10 pm	Hun counter-attacked on Chemical Works.	
		11 pm	Night attack without artillery preparation failed.	
	8th	5 pm	CHINESE barrage.	For orders see App. C.
	10th	9.45 pm	Heavy fire by Divisions on left and right. We opened slow barrage on S.O.S. line for half an hour.	
	11th	4.30 pm	Attack by 4th Division to gain BLACK LINE East of Chemical Works North of ROEUX - carried by 10th Bde. R.F.A. 255th Bde. Lane included chateau in Chemical Works.	For orders see App. D. also barrage map.
		8.35 pm	Objective reported gained - several hundred prisoners - casualties slight.	
	12th	3.30 am	New line for barrage at 6.30 am. See barrage map D.	
		6.30 am	Attack by 4th Division to gain BLUE LINE.	do.

Army Form C. 2118.

WAR DIARY
or
INTELLIGENCE SUMMARY.
(Erase heading not required.)

Instructions regarding War Diaries and Intelligence Summaries are contained in F. S. Regs., Part II. and the Staff Manual respectively. Title pages will be prepared in manuscript.

Place	Date 1917 May	Hour	Summary of Events and Information	Remarks and references to Appendices
PONT DU JOUR	12th	8.30 am	Offensive reported gained - a few prisoners.	initialled
		6 pm	Smoke barrage by B. & C. Batteries to cover attack by VI Corps South of SCARPE.	initialled for orders see Apx. E.
	13th	4.30 pm	S.O.S. which resulted in nothing.	initialled
	14th	4 pm	2 men killed and 1 wounded in A Battery.	initialled
	15th	8 pm	A Battery moved a section to position South of SCARPE at H.27.d. central.	initialled
		9 pm	Patrols found CARROT - CYPRUS +c trenches occupied.	initialled
	16th	3.30 am	S.O.S. enemy attacked Chemical Works and ROEUX.	initialled
		7.15 am	Report from liaison that we had been driven back to West of Chemical Works and out of trenches but were still in ROEUX.	initialled
		8.30 am	Counter attack by 152nd Infantry Bde. on Chemical Works - from this line onward till dusk Infantry gradually drove enemy back and re-established themselves in line held the previous night as far as ground lies between Railway and River. D/255 Ammunition blown up by shell fire - 2500 rounds destroyed and all guns but one out of action. - about 15 casualties.	
	16th	3.30 am	} A. B. & C. Batteries firing almost continuously on various targets.	initialled
	17th	to 3.30 am		
			A/255 in action S. of River SCARPE.	initialled
	19th	7.30 pm	B/255 took part in attack by VI Corps S. of River SCARPE which was unsuccessful.	initialled
	25th		B/255 were heavily shelled and had 2 guns destroyed - only 1 casualty.	initialled
	30th	11.30 pm	B/255 took part in attack by VI Corps S. of River SCARPE which was unsuccessful.	initialled
	31st		Batteries in action N. of ATHIES. Wagon lines at ANZIN.	initialled

initialled
Lt. Col. R.& A.Y.
Commanding 255th (Highland) Bde. R.F.A.

Secret.

CONFD. 4th
No 21 A
HIGHLAND
DIVISION.

War Diary   b 25

of

255th (High'd) Bde. R.F.A. 2

for month of

June 1917.

WAR DIARY
INTELLIGENCE SUMMARY
(Erase heading not required.)

Army Form C. 2118.

Place	Date	Hour	Summary of Events and Information	Remarks and references to Appendices
POINT-DU-JOUR	1917 June 1st		Batteries in action:- A south of the SCARPE. B.C. & D north East of ATHIES. Wagon lines in ANZIN.	
	2nd	10 pm	D Battery moved across SCARPE to FEUCHY.	initialled
	3rd	10 am	Brigade came under orders of 9th Divisional Artillery.	initialled
	4th	10 pm	North end of Hqrs. Mess blown in by shell and Lieut. A.S. Jameson Orderly Officer wounded.	initialled
		11 am	B Battery signal dug-out blown in - one man killed one wounded.	
		2 pm to 8 pm	D Battery shelled: Ammunition blown up: 6 men wounded.	initialled
	5th	8 pm	Attack from junction of CROOK and CHAPLIN on the North to bend in sunken road North East of ROEUX (I.14.c.5.4.) by 9th Division. Attack successful	initialled Appendix A
	6th	10 pm	D Battery moved back to former position in road North of ATHIES.	initialled
	7th	8 pm to 1 am	Enemy very jumpy - also our own Infantry - several S.O.S. calls.	initialled
	8th	11 am	Brigade exchanged positions and zones with 51st Brigade R.F.A. All Batteries now together North of Happy Valley. A.B. & C. in line along a track. D 150 yards behind. Brigade came under orders of 34th Divisional Artillery.	initialled Appendix B

Army Form C. 2118.

WAR DIARY
INTELLIGENCE SUMMARY.
(Erase heading not required.)

Place	Date 1917	Hour	Summary of Events and Information	Remarks and references to Appendices
POINT-DU-JOUR	June 18th	9pm	Brigade relieved by 79th Brigade. Wagon lines moved to SAUSAGE lines South of ACQ.	
	19th	1am	men from gun line arrived at wagon lines.	
ACQ	20th to 30th		Brigade refitting in wagon lines. Guns at I.O.M. Workshops.	

Mundyear
Lieut Col R.F.A.
Commanding 255th (Highland) Bde. R.F.A.

Secret. 51st

Vol 29

**CONFIDENTIAL
No 31 (A)
HIGHLAND
DIVISION.**

War Diary

— of —

255th Brigade R.F.A.

— for month of —

October 1917.

WAR DIARY

INTELLIGENCE SUMMARY

Army Form C. 2118.

Place	Date 1917	Hour	Summary of Events and Information	Remarks and references to Appendices
CANAL BANK	Oct. 1st		A & C/255 moved remainder of Batteries forward to positions near River STEEN BEEK.	
	2nd		B & D/255 Do.	
			2/Lieut. DICKINSON (B/255) killed. Lieut. WRIGHT (A/255) wounded.	
	3rd		2/Lieuts. NEILSON and THOMPSON (C/255) wounded.	
	4th		2nd and 5th ARMIES attacked at 6 am. All objectives gained at 9.45 am on 11th Division front.	
			2/Lieut. FINDLAY (B/255) died of wounds while acting as F.O.O.	
	6th		B/298 relieved C/298 and came under orders of this Brigade.	
	9th		11th Division attacked at 5.20 am - unsuccessful.	
	11th	10 am	18th Div. Arty. take over from 11th D.A. 82nd Bde. R.F.A. take over left Group from 59th Bde. R.F.A.	
	12th		18th Div. attacked at 5.25 am. unsuccessful. 2/Lieut. HEMSLEY (C/255) F.O.O. killed	
	13th	12 noon	34th (A.) Bde. R.F.A. took over "D" Group consisting of that Bde. and 255th Brigade R.F.A.	
	16th		B.C's of 161st Bde. R.F.A. arrive to take over.	
	17th	5 pm	Batteries of 161st Bde. R.F.A. relieve Batteries of 255th Bde. R.F.A.	
	18th		Hqrs. 161st Bde. R.F.A. relieve Hqrs. 255th Bde. R.F.A.	
	19th	12 noon	A/255 entrained at HOPOUTRE at 11.35 am. B/255 at 3.35 pm. C/255 at 8 pm. D/255 at 12 midnight	
POPERINGHE	19th			
	20th		Hqrs. 255th Bde. R.F.A. entrained at 6.30 am and arrived at ACHEUX at 5.30 pm.	
ACHEUX	21st		Brigade billeted. Hqrs & A & B & C/255 at ACHEUX. D/255 at LEALVILLERS.	
	22nd		all guns and hows. sent in to Ordnance ALBERT.	
	24th		5 officers and 29 other ranks reinforcements posted to Brigade.	
	28th		All guns and hows. sent to FRICOURT Range to be calibrated. A/255 moved to FORCEVILLE.	
	29th		C.R.A. inspected the Brigade.	
	31st		Brigade refitting at ACHEUX. A/255 moved to FORCEVILLE.	

Fleming
Commanding 255th (Highland) Bde. R.F.A.

War Diary 51st
of
255th Bde R.F.A.
for month of
November. 1917

CONFIDENTIAL
No 81(A)
HIGHLAND DIVISION.

WAR DIARY
INTELLIGENCE SUMMARY
(Erase heading not required.)

Army Form C. 2118.

Place	Date Nov.	Hour	Summary of Events and Information	Remarks and references to Appendices
ACHEUX	1st		Brigade refitting.	
BOIRY ST MARTIN	3rd		Brigade marched out of ACHEUX area and arrived at Aerodrome Camp at 3 p.m.	
	5th		Advance parties sent to dig positions in HAVRINCOURT Wood.	
ACHEUX	6th		Brigade left Aerodrome Camp and returned to billets in ACHEUX area.	
COURCELLES	14th	4 p.m.	Brigade marched from ACHEUX to COURCELLES.	
BEAULENCOURT	15th	4 p.m.	Brigade marched from COURCELLES to BEAULENCOURT.	
BUS	17th	4 p.m.	Brigade marched from BEAULENCOURT to BUS.	
HAVRINCOURT Wood	18th		Brigade went into action on Eastern edge of HAVRINCOURT Wood.	
	20th	6.20am	III & IV Corps attacked. Tanks and cavalry assisted in strength. Objectives nearly all gained.	
		By 2 p.m.	51st Division held up at FLESQUIERES.	
FLESQUIERES	21st		51st Division took FLESQUIERES early and CANTAING and FONTAINE later. Batteries moved forward into action N.E. of FLESQUIERES.	
"	22nd	10.0am	Boche counter attacked and drove us out of FONTAINE.	
"	23rd	10.30am	40th and 51st Divisions attacked BOURLON Wood and FONTAINE. Attack not successful.	
"	24th		Guards Division relieved 51st Division.	
"	27th	6.20am	62nd Division and Guards Division attacked BOURLON Wood and FONTAINE. Attack successful at first but enemy counter attack drove us back to original line.	
"	28th		59th Division relieved Guards Division.	
"	30th	8 am.	Heavy enemy attacks on left and right of CORPS front. On our Divisional front no enemy attack was made, though enemy shelled Divisional area heavily all day.	

Hemming
Lieut. Col. R.F.A.
Commanding 255th (Highland) Bde. R.F.A.

Secret.

Vol 31

CONFIDENTIAL.
No 31 (A)
HIGHLAND
DIVISION.

War Diary
of
255th (Highland) Brigade R.F.A.
for month of
December 1917.

Army Form C. 2118.

WAR DIARY
— of —
INTELLIGENCE SUMMARY.
(Erase heading not required.)

Instructions regarding War Diaries and Intelligence Summaries are contained in F. S. Regs., Part II. and the Staff Manual respectively. Title pages will be prepared in manuscript.

Place	Date	Hour	Summary of Events and Information	Remarks and references to Appendices
	1917 Dec.			
FLESQUIERES	1st	12 noon	Brigade in action at FLESQUIERES. Hqrs. in sunken road on West side of Village. Lieut. Miles joined as reinforcement.	
	2nd		Attacks from left of BOURLON to MOEUVRES by enemy. Brigade comes under 59th D.A.	
			C/255 move one section to their night car.	
	3rd		C/255 moved remaining sections to new positions.	
	4th		Orders received for Brigade to shift to positions behind FLESQUIERES. B+ D/255 withdrew at 6 p.m.	
			C/255 at 10 p.m. A/255 at 5 a.m. Hqrs. at 5.15 a.m.	
GRAND RAVINE	5th		Batteries in new positions. Infantry withdrew to FLESQUIERES line. Boche attacked at ORIVAL WOOD but was driven back.	
	10th		Exchange of Wound between 59th and 51st Batteries commences — 1 section per Battery. B.C.'s and one officer and the Adjutant change over.	
	11th		Second section of Batteries take over. Major Garden B/255 leaves Brigade to command Rest Camp DOULLENS.	
BEAUMETZ	12th	2.5 p.m.	Relief by Hqrs. and Batteries complete with 295th Bde. R.F.A. O.C. Brigade took over command of Right Group, 51st Div. Arty at 4 p.m. consisting of 255th Bde. R.F.A. and 280th Bde. R.F.A. (51st Division)	
LES CAMIERS			280th Brigade Hqrs. close on our right.	

2353 Wt. W2544/1454 700,000 5/15 D. D. & L. A.D.S.S./Forms/C. 2118.

Army Form C. 2118.

WAR DIARY
or
INTELLIGENCE SUMMARY.
(Erase heading not required.)

Instructions regarding War Diaries and Intelligence Summaries are contained in F. S. Regs., Part II. and the Staff Manual respectively. Title pages will be prepared in manuscript.

Place	Date	Hour	Summary of Events and Information	Remarks and references to Appendices
	1917 Dec.			
	12th		Major C.G. Fenton arrived to take over D/255.	
	13th		5th Brigade A.F.A. relieve 280th Bde. R.F.A. in Right Group. O.C. Brigade inspects all Battery Positions in Group.	
	14th		Boche places bombed BAPAUME and FREMICOURT.	
	22nd		152nd Infantry Brigade come into our Group and we arrange when the 5th Brigade A.F.A. Wagon lines moved to FREMICOURT in morning.	
	23rd		Major J.W. Alexander arrived to take over B/256. 310th Brigade R.F.A. joined our Group. Right Group now consists of 256th Brigade R.F.A. 5th Brigade A.F.A. and 310th Brigade R.F.A.	
	27th		214th Brigade R.F.A. relieve 310th Brigade R.F.A. 10am Division take over more line further South.	
	28th		Captain J. Scott arrived to take over C/255.	
	29th		Holding the line.	

Lieut. Col. R.F.A.
Commanding 256th (Highland) Brigade R.F.A.

Secret.

Vol 32

War Diary

of

255th (Highland) Bde. R.F.A.T.

for month of

January 1918

WAR DIARY
or
INTELLIGENCE SUMMARY

Army Form C. 2118.

Place	Date 1919	Hour	Summary of Events and Information	Remarks and references to Appendices
BEAUMETZ	Jan. 4		Brigade in action. O.C. Brigade commanding Right Group 5th D.A. consisting of 211th Bde. R.F.A. 255 Bde. R.F.A.Y. and 5th (Army) Bde. R.F.A.	Own
"	13th		5th (Army) Bde. R.F.A. withdrew. B/255 took over 6th Battery position near HERMIES.	Own
"	15th		A/255 occupied new position S. of HERMIES.	Own
"	17th		G.O.C. IV Corps (Lt. Gen. Woollcombe) went round Batteries.	Own
"	18		6th Division relieved 5th Division in the line.	Own
"	19th		G.O.C. 3rd Army (Gen. Byng) visited Batteries.	Own
"	21st	12 noon	O.C. 2nd Div. Bde. R.F.A. took over command of Right Group 6th R.A.	Own
"	22nd	5 pm	293rd (Army) Bde. R.F.A. relieved 255th Bde. R.F.A. who proceeded to Argon going to FREMICOURT.	Own
AVESNES	23rd	10 am	Brigade marched from FREMICOURT to AVESNES and were billeted there.	Own
MAILLY MAILLET	24th	10 am	Brigade marched to MAILLY MAILLET and FORCEVILLE (A/255) and were billeted there.	Own
AUTHIE	25th	10 am	Brigade marched to AUTHIE and ST LEGER (B/255) and were billeted there.	Own
"	30th		Guns & howitzers of Brigade proceeded to FRICOURT Range to be calibrated.	Own
"	31st		Brigade resting. Letting up dull - wearing clothes etc. being carried out.	Own

Ashton Major R.H.A.?
Commanding 255th (Highland) Bde. R.F.A.Y.

Secret.

War Diary

of

255th (Highland) Bde. R.F.A.T.

for month of

February 1918.

WAR DIARY
or
INTELLIGENCE SUMMARY.
(Erase heading not required.)

Army Form C. 2118.

Place	Date 1918	Hour	Summary of Events and Information	Remarks and references to Appendices
AUTHIE	July 1st		BRIGADE at rest. Training, drilling etc. being carried out.	Ann
	4th		Completion of calibration of Guns at FRICOURT RANGE and return of party	Ann
	8th		G.O.C. R.A., III Army inspected billets and horse lines.	Ann
BOUZINCOURT	12th	10 a.m.	Brigade marched to BOUZINCOURT and now billeted there.	Ann
	13th		One section for Battery relieved one Section for Battery of 241st Brigade R.F.A. in the line. 51st (Highland) Division relieved 6th Division.	Ann
BEAUMETZ	14th		Wagon lines of Brigade marched to FREMICOURT. Remainder of Gun Line personnel proceeded by motor lorries to BEAUMETZ. Brigade relieved 241st Brigade R.F.A. in the line and came under orders of O.C. 293rd (Army) Brigade R.F.A. Commanding Right Group 51st D.A.	Ann
	20th		Batteries commenced digging reinforcing positions.	Ann
	24th		O.C. 255th Brigade R.F.A. took over command of Right Group 51st D.A. consisting of 255th Brigade R.F.A. and 293rd (Army) Brigade R.F.A.	Ann
	28th		Brigade in action - just N.E. of BEAUMETZ.	Ann

Young Lieut. Col. R.F.A.Y.
Commanding 255th (Highland) Bde. R.F.A.Y.

51st Divisional Artillery

WAR DIARY

255th BRIGADE

ROYAL FIELD ARTILLERY

MARCH 1918

Army Form C. 2118.

CONFIDENTIAL

WAR DIARY

of

255th Brigade R.F.A.

From 1.3.18 to 31.3.18

Instructions regarding War Diaries and Intelligence Summaries are contained in F.S. Regs., Part II. and the Staff Manual respectively. Title pages will be prepared in manuscript.

Place	Date 1918	Hour		Remarks and references to Appendices
BEAUMETZ	1st MARCH		Brigade in action at	
"	8th "		7th A.v.S.H. raided line	
"	21/st "	5 A.M.	Enemy attacked under	
		10 A.M.	BEAUMETZ - MORCHIES L[ine]	
			STURGEON Av. ill. and	
			20 missing. B. v C/255	
			Brigade lost 17 18—[?]	
			[south]part S. of BEUGN[Y]	
			BEAUMETZ - MORCHIES LI[NE]	
LEBUCQUIÈRE	22nd "	4 A.M.	H.Qrs. moved back to S[?]	
			+ attacked but was d[...]	
			BEAUMETZ - MORCHIES R[...]	
			HERMIES to CAMBRAI R[oad]	
FREMICOURT	23rd "	1 A.M.	H.Qrs. moved back to [...]	
			each 4 B/255 with 5 [...]	
RIENCOURT	"	12 noon	H.Qrs + Batteries with	
		10 A.M.	BEUGNY	
THILLOY	24th "		H.Qrs + Batteries with	
ACHIET-LE-PETIT	"	11 P.M.	H.Qrs + Batteries with	
PUISEAUX	25th "	9 A.M.	" " came	
SERRE	"	4 p.m.	" " came	
FONQUEVILLERS	"	12 M.N.	" " with[...]	
BIENVILLERS	26th "	10 A.M.	" " with[...]	
LA SOUICH	27th "	2 p.m.	Brigade Rested to LA [...]	
"	28th "	10 A.M.	Brigade marched to W[...]	
WAIL	29th "	11 A.M.	" " to HE[...]	
	31/03			

WAR DIARY
INTELLIGENCE SUMMARY.
(Erase heading not required.)

Army Form C. 2118.

Instructions regarding War Diaries and Intelligence Summaries are contained in F. S. Regs., Part II. and the Staff Manual respectively. Title pages will be prepared in manuscript.

N/A 34.

Place	Date 1918	Hour	Summary of Events and Information	Remarks and references to Appendices
BEAUMETZ	March 7th		Brigade in action at BEAUMETZ-LEZ-CAMBRAI	
"	8th		7th A.v.S.H. raided enemy outpost line & found it unoccupied	
"	9/3	5 A.M.	Enemy attacked under cover of very heavy barrage of 5.9" & 4.2"s. Made rapid progress on L/f. At 8 a.m. had possession of our intermediate line N. of Cambrai Road & at North was in front of BEAUMETZ-MORCHIES LINE. DOIGNIES was captured by 2 p.m. but right of Division held out along STURGEON AV. till dusk. Brigade casualties - Officers 2 killed, 8 wounded. O.Rs. 5 killed, 23 wounded. 20 missing. B & C/255 positions captured by enemy by 1 p.m. Also all forward anti-tank guns. Brigade lost 17 18-pdr. destroyed or captured & 1 How. B/255 withdrew at 5 p.m. Thro' guns to a position S. of BEUGNY under a heavy barrage. At 5 p.m. enemy opened heavy barrage on Brigade position BEAUMETZ-MORCHIES LINE & back area, then attacked but was repulsed. A.B.&C/255 out of action. BEAUMETZ-MORCHIES LINE to CAMBRAI Road.	
LEBUCQUIÈRE	22nd	4 A.M.	H.Qrs. moved back to SAPPER CAMP. At 5 p.m. barrage who again opened & enemy penetrated & attacked but was repulsed. At 10 A.M. enemy opened heavy barrage on BEAUMETZ-MORCHIES LINE & CAMBRAI Road. Divisional front now run behind BEAUMETZ from HERMIES to CAMBRAI Road.	
FREMICOURT	23rd	1 A.M.	H.Qrs moved back to Old Div. Hqrs. Infantry now holding Corps line A & C/255 in action with 2 guns each & B/255 with 5 Hows. at MILL CROSS. FREMICOURT heavily shelled from 1 A.m. to 12 noon. H.Qrs & Batteries withdrew to pt. E. of RIENCOURT & Batteries came into action covering FREMICOURT	
RIENCOURT	"	12 noon	H.Qrs. & Batteries withdrew to pt. E. of THILLOY & Batteries came into action covering FREMICOURT	
THILLOY	24th	10 A.m.	H.Qrs. & Batteries withdrew to pt. E. of THILLOY & Batteries came into action at ACHIET-LE-PETIT.	
ACHIET-LE-PETIT	"	11 P.M.	H.Qrs & Batteries withdrew to position of readiness at BEAUREGARD DOVECOT covering our line E. of LOUPART WOOD.	
PUISEAUX	25th	9 A.m.	" " came into action at BEAUREGARD DOVECOT covering our line E. of LOUPART WOOD.	
SERRE	"	4 p.m.	" " came into action W. of SERRE.	
FONQUEVILLERS	"	12 M.N.	" " withdrew to position of readiness at FONQUEVILLERS	
BIENVILLERS	26th	10 A.m.	" " withdrew to LA CAUCHIE & at 7 p.m. moved forward to BIENVILLERS & joined up with Wagon Lines.	
LA SOUICH	27th	2 p.m.	Brigade Rested	
"	28th	10 A.m.	Brigade marched to LA SOUICH	
WAIL	29th	11 A.m.	" " to WAIL	
"	3/4		" " to HERLIN LE SEC.	

Signed [signature]
Lt.-Col. R.A.
O.C. 255 Bde R.F.A.

51st Divisional Artillery

WAR DIARY

255th (Highland) BRIGADE

ROYAL FIELD ARTILLERY

APRIL 1 9 1 8

Secret.

War Diary

— of —

255th (Highland) Bde. R.F.A.

— for month of —

April 1918.

Army Form C. 2118.

WAR DIARY
or
INTELLIGENCE SUMMARY.
(Erase heading not required.)

Instructions regarding War Diaries and Intelligence Summaries are contained in F. S. Regs., Part II. and the Staff Manual respectively. Title pages will be prepared in manuscript.

Place	Date 1918	Hour	Summary of Events and Information	Remarks and references to Appendices
HAILLICOURT	April 1st/3rd	2 P.M.	Brigade arrived from HERLIN-LE-SEC and were billeted.	
"	4th		Brigade training.	
AMETTES	5th	11 A.M.	Brigade marched to & billeted at AMETTES.	
"	8th		Brigade refitting - Positions reconnoitred near BULLY GRENAY to reinforce 46th Div.	
PARADIS	9th	7/15 A.M.	Brigade alarmed. Stood to all hoop. Then marched to CORNET MALO (Q28) Batteries came into action for 7 P.M. South of PARADIS covering line between VIEILLE CHAPELLE and LESTREM, less A/51st Div. in withdrawal.	
"	10th		Batteries fired throughout the day chiefly on bridges over R. LAWE. During the evening enemy forced a crossing over the R. LAWE near LESTREM. Rules reported at 1 A.M. advancing in direction of BATTERIES.	
RIEZ-DU-VINAGE	11th	11 A.M.	H.Q. + Batteries moved. MG fire to position just E. of PACAUT WOOD. B Coy- came into action there.	
"		2 P.M.	Batteries withdrew to position South of RIEZ DU VINAGE reporting to CO W.I.Cs. Batteries were without any warning fired on by enemy infantry at 300 yds. range. The Batteries suddenly found there had been infantry attacking on their left flank at very close range. CO (Lieut Col Rundon DSO TD) with A/Stallion Officer with 152 Bde R.F.A was taken prisoner along with the 2nd Bde Staff Casualties were 10 wounded, 1 missing, 1 OR killed. 15 OR wounded.	
BUSNES	12th	5 A.M.	18 pdrs of 2 + 15 How. lost. Captured by the enemy. Remainder of Brigade withdrew under very heavy L.T.M.G. Fire which was returned. R.A. position half mile SE of BUSNES covering ROBECQ wat the exception of 3 18pdrs which were knocked out & put the LA BASSEE CANAL struggled to the arrival of unknown reinforcements, 2 Officers + 40 Other ranks were used to defend the canal bank until the arrival of the infantry reinforced by 51st Div. at 10 AM on 13th. A patrol went out during the afternoon of 12th reached the bridges on the loop 13th Divn by rifle fire.	
L'ECLEME	15th		H.Q. + Batteries moved forward to positions S. of LA BASSÉE CANAL near ROBECQ 4th Divn attached. Reoccupied RIEZ-DU-VINAGE 3. 4.5 Hows. + 5 18pdrs + Brewelse of 3 18-pdrs. 5 and 4. Brigade covering the Divn.	
"	21st		Major T. Rawdon D.S.O. took over command of Brigade vice Lt Col Fleming DSO TD missing.	
"	23rd		Lt Col Rawdon attached & gained all objectives with 1 Off + 15 O.Rs. prisoners.	
"	24th		Enemy counter-attacked unsuccessfully losing 5 Offs + 120 O.Rs.	
"	30th		Brigade in action S. of ROBECQ	

T. Rawdon

A/Colonel RFA
Commanding 255th (Highland) Brigade RFA

Secret

War Diary
— of —
255th (High.) Bde. R.F.A.
— for month of —
May 1918

Army Form C. 2118.

WAR DIARY
or
INTELLIGENCE=SUMMARY.
(Erase heading not required.)

Instructions regarding War Diaries and Intelligence Summaries are contained in F. S. Regs., Part II. and the Staff Manual respectively. Title pages will be prepared in manuscript.

Place	Date	Hour	Summary of Events and Information	Remarks and references to Appendices
L'ECLEME	1918 May 1st		4 other ranks wounded.	T.W.
	2nd		Chinese barrage at 10 p.m.	T.W.
	8th		4 Officers and 16 other ranks from 52nd Division attached.	T.W.
	9th		A/255's farm destroyed by shell fire.	T.W.
	10th		B Battery position shelled and farm destroyed.	T.W.
	11th		A Battery shelled - no damage.	T.W.
	12th		A Battery moved back 1000 yards.	T.W.
	13th		Raid by 61st Division - 2 prisoners taken - no casualties to raiding party. Barrage by 255 and 256 Bdes	T.W.
	14th		" " " - 1 prisoner taken.	T.W.
	19th/20th		Brigade interchanging positions with 309th Bde. 1 section per 18 Pdr. Battery taken over	T.W.
	20th		" " "	T.W.
	21st		Interchange with 309th Brigade completed. 255th Brigade in Left Group, 4th Div. Artillery.	J.T.W.
	31st		Group consists of 29th Brigade R.F.A. and 255th (Highland) Bde. R.F.A. Brigade still in action S. of ROBECQ.	T.W.

T. Davidson Lieut. Col. R.F.A.
Commanding 255th (Highland) Bde. R.F.A.

Secret.

War Diary

— of —

255th (Highland) Bde. R.F.A.

— for month of —

June 1918.

Army Form C. 2118.

WAR DIARY
—or—
INTELLIGENCE=SUMMARY.
(Erase heading not required.)

Place	Date 1918	Hour	Summary of Events and Information	Remarks and references to Appendices
L'ECLEME	June 1st		Brigade in action covering 4th Division.	Com
	3rd		One Section per Battery of 65th (Army) Bde. R.F.A. relieved one section per Battery of 255th (Highld.) Bde. R.F.A.	Com
	4th	10.30 a.m.	65th (Army) Bde. R.F.A. relieved 255th Bde in the line. Brigade marched to ESTREE CAUCHIE.	Com
ESTREE CAUCHIE	5th	7 a.m.	Brigade went into billets at ESTREE CAUCHIE in 1st Army Reserve.	Com
	6th		Brigade refitting.	Com
MADAGASCAR	16th		Brigade marched to temporary Wagon Lines at MADAGASCAR. Half Batteries took over from 40th Bde. R.F.A.	Com
ROCLINCOURT	17th	10 h.m.	Brigade relieved 70th Bde. R.F.A. in the line, covering Right Infy. Bde, 5th Division.	Com
	21st	3 a.m.	Brigade supported successful raid by 13th Royal Scots (15th Division) who took 10 prisoners.	Com
	22nd		Wagon Lines took over from 41st Bde. R.F.A. (2nd Division)	Com
	24th		Epidemic ("3 days Fever") started in Brigade.	Com
	29th		120 all ranks down with epidemic. Raid by 1/7th Black Watch at 11.10 p.m. No identifications secured.	Com
	30th		Brigade in action near ROCLINCOURT covering Right Infy. Bde. 51st (Highland) Division	Com

J. Sanders Lieut. Col. R.F.A.Y.
Commanding 255th (Highland) Bde. R.F.A.Y.

Divisional Artillery

51st (Highland) Division.

255th BRIGADE R. F. A.

J U L Y 1918

Vol 38

War Diary.
— of —
255th Bde. R.F.A.
— for month of —
July 1918

Army Form C. 2118.

WAR DIARY
or
INTELLIGENCE SUMMARY.
(Erase heading not required.)

Instructions regarding War Diaries and Intelligence Summaries are contained in F. S. Regs., Part II. and the Staff Manual respectively. Title pages will be prepared in manuscript.

Place	Date 1918	Hour	Summary of Events and Information	Remarks and references to Appendices
ROCLINCOURT	11th July		Brigade in action covering 51st (Highland) Division.	—
	12th "		Section for Battery relieved by 3rd Canadian F.A. Bde.	—
	13th "	11 P.M.	Bt Com H.Q. Bde relieved 255 Bde R.F.A. in the Line.	—
LA COMTÉ	14th "		Brigade marched to LA COMTÉ. 3rd Can Div relieved 51st Div in the Line.	—
PERNES	15th "		Brigade entrained at PERNES.	—
LA CHAPELLE	16th "		H.Q. detrained at PONT-SUR-SEINE & marched to LA CHAPELLE. A/255 detrained at HERMÉ & marched to ALLEMAGNE. B/255 detrained at NOGENT & marched to BETHON. C/255 detrained at PONT-SUR-SEINE + B/255 at HERMÉ.	—
			Brigade (less B/255) marched to CLAMANGES. B/255 at BETHON.	—
CLAMANGES	18th "		Brigade (less B/255) marched all night to position S. of NANTEUIL-LA-FOSSE arriving there at 6 A.M.	—
BOIS LE ST. QUENTIN	19th "		Brigade (less B/255) in action S. of NANTEUIL covering 51st Division in General attack. 62nd Div. (English) on Right of our Div. (French) on left. 51st Divs advanced 1 kilo. & took about 400 pr'soners	—
	20th "	8 A.M.	Bty.de supported attack by Left By. Bde. 5th Div in minor attack. B/255 in action N. of NANTEUIL-LA-FOSSE	—
	21st "	6 A.M.	Batteries moved to N. of NANTEUIL-LA-FOSSE + supported attack by 51st Div. who advanced 500 yds + took 40 prisoners.	—
	23rd "	6 A.M.	H.Qrs. moved to NANTEUIL.	—
NANTEUIL-LA-FOSSE	24th "		51st Div attacked at 6 A.M. All objectives gained by 9 A.M. without opposition. Enemy apparently in retreat	—
	27th "	2 p.m.	H.Qrs. moved to POURCY. Batteries to MARFAUX area.	—
			Enemy still retreating followed by our troops. B/255 moved forward to N. of CHAUMUZY.	—
POURCY	28th "			—
ST IMOGES	30th "	12 noon	Brigade withdrew from action + bivouacked for the night at ST IMOGES.	—
EPERNAY	31st "		H.Qrs. entrained at 3 P.M. B/255 at 7 P.M. at EPERNAY. A.C. + B/255 in Wagon Lines at ST IMOGES.	—

Commanding 255th (High'd) Bde R.F.A.T.

To Lt Colonel R.F.A.T.
Commanding 255th (High'd) Bde R.F.A.T.

Secret

War Diary

of

255th (Highland) Bde. R.F.A.T.

for month of

August 1918.

WAR DIARY
or
INTELLIGENCE SUMMARY.
(Erase heading not required.)

Army Form C. 2118.

Instructions regarding War Diaries and Intelligence Summaries are contained in F. S. Regs., Part II. and the Staff Manual respectively. Title pages will be prepared in manuscript.

Place	Date	Hour	Summary of Events and Information	Remarks and references to Appendices
ACQ	1918 August 1st		Headqrs. and Batteries detrained at BRUAS and PERNES and marched to billets at ACQ	Cttm
"	2nd		Brigade refitting and training	Cttm
"	8th		H.M. The King passed through ACQ.	Cttm
"	11th		Indn Brigade Competition for Turnout won by A/255.	Cttm
"	14th		3 guns per battery relieved similar number of 56th Bde. R.F.A. (52nd Division) in ROCLINCOURT area	Cttm
ROCLINCOURT	15th		255th Brigade R.F.A relieved 56th Bde R.F.A. covering 154th Infantry Brigade (51st Division)	Cttm
"	20th		Batteries moved forward to BOIS de la MAISON BLANCHE area.	Cttm
"	21st	1.30am	Brigade assisted in an attack by 152nd Infy. Bde. on night of Arleux front (unsuccessful)	Cttm
			Division Corps under Canadian Corps at 12 noon.	Cttm
BOIS de la MAISON BLANCHE	23rd		Headqrs. moved to gun pits in Railway Cutting.	Cttm
"	24th	6 am	Brigade resisted unsuccessful attack by 153rd Infantry Bde.	Cttm
"	25th	6 am	Brigade again assisted unsuccessful minor operation by 153rd Infy. Bde.	Cttm
"	26th	3 am	2nd & 3rd Canadian Divisions attacked on our right and gained all objectives by 11 am including MONCHY,	Cttm
			255th Bde. assisted with barrage N. of River Scarpe.	Cttm
		10.30 am	51st Division attacked and gained all objectives including on and taking Mt. PLEASANT WOOD and CHEMICAL WORKS, ROEUX.	Cttm
		4 pm	152nd & 153rd Infy. Bdes. attacked, gaining all objectives. GAVRELLE taken during night 26/27.	Cttm
			Batteries moved forward to POINT DU JOUR area	Cttm
"	29th	10 am	153rd Infy. Bde. attacked GREENLAND HILL but failed to hold on. 8th Division relieved	Cttm
			154th Infy. Bde. at midnight. Hqrs. moved to MUSKETRY VALLEY.	Cttm

Army Form C. 2118.

WAR DIARY
or
INTELLIGENCE SUMMARY.
(Erase heading not required.)

Instructions regarding War Diaries and Intelligence Summaries are contained in F. S. Regs., Part II. and the Staff Manual respectively. Title pages will be prepared in manuscript.

Place	Date 1918	Hour	Summary of Events and Information	Remarks and references to Appendices
MUSKETRY VALLEY	August 28th	12 noon	2/Lieut. J. Duncan and 12 other ranks formed arm'd patrol which reconnoitred ground between river Scarpe and GREENLAND HILL and confirmed that HAUSA and DELBAR WOODS were held by the enemy.	Apm Capm Capm
	29th	6.30 a.m.	154th Inf. Bde. attacked GREENLAND HILL and gained objective with 40 prisoners. Into HAUSA and DELBAR Woods reached by patrols of 152nd Inf. Bde. Batteries moved forward. A. & B/255 Cam to West of ROEUX Chez. and B & D/255 to FAMPOUX. 51st Div Cam under 22nd Corps at 12 noon	Capm
	30th	4 pm	H/hm Brigade carried crossing 154th Inf. Bde. which they had done since 15th inst and now cover 152nd Inf. Bde. 6th Dandries at Junion with B.G.C., 152nd Inf. Bde.	Capm Capm Capm
	31st		B & D/255 moved forward to MT PLEASANT Wood. Brigade in action covering 152nd Inf. Bde. in PLOUVAIN Section.	Capm Capm

Crowton Capt & Adj.

for Lieut Col. R.F.A.Y.
Commanding 255th (Highland) Brigade R.F.A.Y.

SECRET.

WAR DIARY

- of -

255th (Highland) Brigade R.F.A.T.

for month of

SEPTEMBER, 1918.

Army Form C. 2118.

WAR DIARY
INTELLIGENCE SUMMARY.
(Erase heading not required.)

Instructions regarding War Diaries and Intelligence Summaries are contained in F. S. Regs., Part II. and the Staff Manual respectively. Title pages will be prepared in manuscript.

Place	Date 1918	Hour	Summary of Events and Information	Remarks and references to Appendices
MUSKETRY VALLEY	Septr. 1st		Brigade in action West of ROEUX, covering Right Infantry Brigade (152 Bde.) 51st Division.	Capt.
	3rd		A.B. & B/255 withdrew H guns for Battery to rear positions N. of CAM VALLEY.	Capt.
	6th		Lieut. Col. H. ALLCARD, A.D.O., R.F.A., resumed temporary command of 255th Bde. R.F.A., during absence of Lieut. Col. J. Davidson, D.S.O., R.F.A. J.	Capt.
CAM VALLEY	11th		Hqrs. moved to CAM VALLEY alongside 152 Infantry Bde. Hqrs.	Capt.
	12th		One Section per Battery of 245th Brigade R.F.A. (Hqt. Division) relieved ditto of 255th Bde R.F.A. in the line	Capt.
	13th	4 p.m.	245th Bde. R.F.A. (Hqt. Div.) relieved 255th Bde. R.F.A. in "PLOUVAIN" sector. 255th Bde. R.F.A. proceeded to billets at ACQ.	Capt.
ACQ	14th	10 a.m.	Hqt. (W.R.) Division relieved 51st (Highland) Division in the line N. of the River SCARPE.	Capt.
	15th		Brigade re-equipping.	Capt.
	16th		Intensive Training - Scheme in connection with contact Aeroplanes.	Capt.
	17th		do. - do. - Scheme - supporting Infantry advance.	Capt.
	18th		do. - do. - Scheme - Mobile Anti-Tank tactics.	Capt.
	19th		do. - do. - Scheme - Dealing with enemy M.G. in collaboration with our Infantry.	Capt.
CAM VALLEY	24th	4 p.m.	255th Bde. R.F.A. relieved 245th Bde. R.F.A. (Hqt. Div.) in "PLOUVAIN" sector covering 153 Inf. Bde. (51st Divn.)	Capt.
	25th	10 a.m.	5th (Highland) Division relieved Hqt. (West Riding) Division in the line North of the River SCARPE.	Capt.
	27th	5.35 a.m.	"Chinese" Barrage put down by 51st Div. Artillery in support of successful operations South of the SCARPE and SENSEE Rivers.	Capt.
	28th		A/255 moved forward H guns from rear position to forward position W. of ROEUX. D/255 withdrew	Capt.
			2 howrs. to Wagon lines.	Capt.
	29th		B/255 withdrew H guns from rear positions to Wagon Lines for training purposes.	Capt.

WAR DIARY
INTELLIGENCE SUMMARY
(Erase heading not required.)

Army Form C. 2118.

Place	Date 1918	Hour	Summary of Events and Information	Remarks and references to Appendices
CAM VALLEY	Sept. 29th		B/255 moved forward 2 guns for wire-cutting to position East of CHEMICAL WORKS. 152 Infantry Bde. relieved 153 Infantry Bde. in PLOUVAIN Sector.	Appx. Appx.
	30th		Brigade in action West of ROEUX covering 152 Inf. Bde. (51st Division) in PLOUVAIN Sector. Dispositions as follows:- A/255 6 guns West of ROEUX; B/255 2 guns East of CHEMICAL WORKS, 4 guns in Wagon Lines; C/255 2 guns West of ROEUX, 4 guns North of CAM VALLEY; D/255 2 hows. West of ROEUX, 2 hows West of JIGSAW WOOD, 2 hows South of River SCARPE, 2 hows in Wagon Lines.	Appx. Appx. Appx. Appx. Appx. Appx.

Commun Capt Adj

R. [illegible] Lieut Col. R.F.A.
Commanding 255th (Highland) Bde. R.F.A.

Secret.

War Diary

— of —

255th (Highland) Bde. R.F.A.

— for month of —

October 1918

Army Form C. 2118.

WAR DIARY
INTELLIGENCE SUMMARY.
(Erase heading not required.)

Instructions regarding War Diaries and Intelligence Summaries are contained in F. S. Regs., Part II. and the Staff Manual respectively. Title pages will be prepared in manuscript.

Place	Date 1918 October	Hour	Summary of Events and Information	Remarks and references to Appendices
CAM VALLEY	1st		Brigade in action W. of ROEUX covering 152 Inf. Bde. (51st Division) in PLOUVAIN Sector	Copy
	2nd	00.30	Brigade supported unsuccessful attack by 152 Inf. Bde.	Copy
			One Section per Battery relieved by one Section per Battery of 33rd Bde. R.F.A. (8th Division)	Copy
	3rd	14.00	Brigade relieved by 33rd Bde. R.F.A. (8th Division). B/255 proceeded to join 154 Inf. Bde. at LE PENDU. A/255 joined 153 Inf. Bde. at MADAGASCAR. Hqrs. A & C/255 moved on chief to billets at HABARCQ.	Copy
HABARCQ	4th		Hqrs. A & C/255 training at HABARCQ. B & D/255 training with 154 and 153 Inf. Bde.	Copy
CAGNICOURT	5th		Brigade marched to CAGNICOURT and bivouacked in the open.	Copy
BOURLON	6th		Brigade came into action at RAILLENCOURT under orders of 3rd Canadian D.A. covering left Inf. Bde. of 3rd Canadian Division. Wagon Lines at INCHY.	Copy
	7th		Bde. came under orders of 39th D.A. covering 3rd Canadian Division.	Copy
	8th	04.30	Bde. took part in "Chinese" attack in support of attack on the night of 3rd Army.	Copy
	9th	01.30	Bde. supported attack by 2nd Canadian Division, resulting in the fall of CAMBRAI.	Copy
		18.00	Bde. came out of action and into Canadian bays reserve, remaining in position. Wagon lines moved up to RAILLENCOURT and joined Batteries.	Copy
	10th		Brigade came under orders of 3rd Canadian Division.	Copy
NAVES	11th		Batteries moved forward and came into action just S. of IWUY, covering 2nd Canadian Division. Hqrs. in open W. of NAVES.	Copy
IWUY	12th	00.01	51st Division relieved 2nd Canadian Division. Brigade now covering 152 Inf. Bde. in right Group 51 D.A. consisting of :- (39th D.A.) 174 Bde. R.F.A. 186th Bde. R.F.A. and 255th Bde. R.F.A.	Copy

WAR DIARY
INTELLIGENCE SUMMARY
(Erase heading not required.)

Army Form C. 2118.

Place	Date 1918	Hour	Summary of Events and Information	Remarks and references to Appendices
IWUY	October 12th	12.00	51st Division attacked and gained all objectives by 14.00. Battalion moved forward to positions just S. of AVESNES-LE-SEC - Hqrs. in IWUY. Mobile sections from B/255 under 2/Lieuts. FORSYTH and RALPH did excellent work. 2/Lieut. RALPH died of wounds.	Copy Copy Copy
	13th	09.00	51st Division attacked and were met by very strong opposition from Artillery and M.G. fire. Attack failed. Brigade was in position of readiness as a mobile Brigade and suffered heavily from enemy Artillery fire. Bdr. S.H.WIGG killed, 1 O.R. killed and 25 wounded. 28 horses killed and 18 wounded. Mobile sections of A/255 under 2/Lieut. P.H. UNWIN did magnificent work at WINDMILL in shelling determined enemy counter-attacks and destroying many M.G.s. Battalions withdrew at dusk to positions just E. of IWUY. Cpm	Copy Copy Copy Copy Copy Copy
	14th	0800	Infantry pushed out patrols but found enemy in strength and had to withdraw.	Copy
	15th		Wagon lines moved back to ESCADOEUVRES?	Copy
	19th	1H.00	Enemy started withdrawing on Division front. At 16.00 Battalions were moved forward and came into action at AVESNES-LE-SEC at 18.00. Brigade now covering 154 Inf. Bde.	Copy Copy
AVESNES-LE-SEC NOYELLES-SUR-SELLE	20th	0500	Battalions moved N. of AVESNES. Hqrs. to AVESNES.	Copy
	21st		Battalions moved forward and crossed River SELLE to positions just E. of River. Hqrs. moved to NOYELLES. Enemy withdrew behind the ECAILLON River. 51st Division took THIANT. 255th Bde. R.F.A. took over Right Group, 51 D.A. consisting of 17H & 18Bth Bdes. R.F.A. and 114th (Army) Bde. R.F.A. at 18.00. 153 Inf. Bde. agreed and 154 Inf. Bde. held all Division front.	Copy Copy Copy Copy
	22nd		"Chinese" Barrage fired at 06.45, 09.00, 11.30, and 16.00. 153 Inf. Bde. relieved 154 Inf. Bde. in the line at 18.00.	Copy Copy

WAR DIARY
INTELLIGENCE SUMMARY

Army Form C. 2118.

Place	Date 1918	Hour	Summary of Events and Information	Remarks and references to Appendices
NOYELLES-SUR-SELLE	October 23rd		"Chinese" Barrage at 05·00, 15·00, and 15·45. HHs(a) Bde. formed Right Group, 51 D.A.	
	24th	04·00	51st Division attacked and gained BLUE line by 14·00. Batteries moved forward to positions East of River ECAILLON and were in action there at 16·00. Right Group 51 D.A. now consists of 255th Bde. R.F.A., 186th Bde. R.F.A., 77th and 114th (Army) Bdes. R.F.A. 152 Inf. Bde. took over Right half of 153 Inf. Bde. Zone and were covered by Right Group 51 D.A.	
THIANT	25th	09·00	51st Division attacked and gained all objectives by 11·00. Enemy counter attacked heavily at 16·00 and our troops withdrew to the line of VALENCIENNES - QUESNOY Railway. HQrs. moved to THIANT. Enemy Counter attack was stopped from making further progress by 5th A. & S. Highlanders who met the enemy with the bayonet.	
	26th	10·00	51st Division attacked - all objectives gained on Right Bde. front by 12·00 but Left Bde. held up at MONT HOUY. Batteries moved forward to just S. of MAING. After heavy bombardment enemy counter attacked at 16·00 and drove back some of our troops. Situation restored by 19·00. Over 500 civilians liberated in FAMARS.	
	27th		Situation in front tense all day. "Counter Preparation" fired at 15·00, 19·00 and 22·00.	
	28th		"Counter Preparation" fired at 01·30, and 17·00. Left Bde. (154 Inf. Bde.) attacked at 05·15 and MONT HOUY started taken by 08·30. Situation obscure all day but enemy filtered back and at 18·00 held MONT HOUY again.	
	29th	10·00	149th Division relieved 51st Division (less Artillery) in the line. Command of Right Artillery Group passed to O.C. 246 Bde. R.F.A. (49th D.A.). Batteries moved at dawn to forward positions S. of FAMARS.	
	31st		Bde. in action covering Right Battn. of 149th Bde. (149th Division) in the FAMARS sector.	

(signed) Lieut Col R.F.A.
Commanding 255th (H) Bde. R.F.A.

Secret.

War Diary

— of —

255th (Highland) Bde. R.F.A.

— for month of —

November 1918.

Army Form C. 2118.

WAR DIARY
INTELLIGENCE SUMMARY.

Instructions regarding War Diaries and Intelligence Summaries are contained in F.S. Regs., Part II. and the Staff Manual respectively. Title pages will be prepared in manuscript.

(Erase heading not required.)

Place	Date 1918	Hour	Summary of Events and Information	Remarks and references to Appendices
MAING	Nov. 1st	05.15	22nd bays attacked. Brigade supported Hqs. Division. All objectives gained by 09.00 hours.	J.W.
			2000 prisoners taken.	J.W.
	2nd	05.30	Hqs. Division attacked and gained objectives in minor operation with 400 prisoners.	J.W.
	3rd		Enemy withdrew on Brigade front. Brigade stood fast.	J.W.
SEBOURQUIAX	6th	1900	Brigade came into action East of SEBOURQUIAX covering 63rd Division. Bde. in 63rd Group (Lt. Col. MEIKLE)	J.W.
	7th	0900	63rd Division attacked.	J.W.
ANGRE		1300	Brigade Hqrs. moved to ANGRE. A/255 in action N.E. of ANGRE.	J.W.
	8th	0530	B.b. & D/255 "in position of assembly" N.E. of ANGRE.	J.W.
		0900	Enemy stated to be withdrawing. Brigade following up.	J.W.
WIHERIES		1400	B.b. & D/255 in action in WIHERIES. A/255 2000× E. of WIHERIES. Bde. Hqrs. in WIHERIES.	J.W.
	9th	0100	Brigade pushed on in close support of 63rd Division Infantry. About now D/255 came into action in our front line at SARS LA BRUYERE. Remaining Batteries at 13.00 hours.	J.W.
			In afternoon Batteries continued to push on and at 1700 hours came into action N. of	J.W.
QUEVY LE PETIT		1700	QUEVY LE PETIT. Hqrs. at BOMMETEAU. Total days advance 14000 yards	J.W.
ESQUILLIES	10th	1600	Brigade in support. At dusk moved into action near ESQUILLIES Line of advance switched from due E. to N.E. Enemy resistance stiffening. At 2000 hours others	J.W.

J. Davidson Lt. Col.

Army Form C. 2118.

WAR DIARY
INTELLIGENCE SUMMARY
(Erase heading not required.)

Place	Date 1918	Hour	Summary of Events and Information	Remarks and references to Appendices
ESQUILLIES	Nov. 10th		Orders received that Brigade would interclif South next morning and assist in supporting 189th Infantry Bde. (63rd (R.N.) Division).	J.D.
	11th	0600	Batteries moving South. When G.O. was reporting to B.G.C. 189th Infantry Bde at 0830 hours orders received that an armistice would take effect at 1100 hours. Brigade pushed on and	J.D.
	11th	1100	took up defensive positions before 1100 hours in GIVRY. D/255 first Battery to reach GIVRY. Warning Order received that Divisional Artillery would march forward shortly into Germany	J.D.
GIVRY			as part of XXII Corps.	J.D.
	16th		G.O.C. 51st Division inspected and addressed Brigade.	J.D.
	17th to 27th		Brigade shifting.	J.D.
	28th	-	Brigade moved from GIVRY at 0900 hours and billeted in ROEULX at 1400 hours.	J.D.
ROEULX	30th		Brigade at ROEULX.	J.D.

J. Davidson Lieut. Col. R.F.A.
Commanding 255th (Highland) Brigade R.F.A.

Confidential

War Diary

of

255th Bde R.F.A.

for

December, 1918.

Army Form C. 2118.

WAR DIARY
or
INTELLIGENCE SUMMARY.
(Erase heading not required.)

Instructions regarding War Diaries and Intelligence Summaries are contained in F. S. Regs., Part II. and the Staff Manual respectively. Title pages will be prepared in manuscript.

Place	Date	Hour	Summary of Events and Information	Remarks and references to Appendices
ROEULX.	1918 1st to 31st Decr.		Brigade in Billets in ROEULX. Educational training carried out under Battery arrangements.	Cm
			Demobilisation of Coal Miners and Pivotal Men commenced on 13th December and during the month the following were demobilised :-	Cm
			28 Miners, 4 Policemen, 2 Pivotal and 3 for length of Service in the Field.	Cm Cm
			Recreational training carried out, the Final in the Brigade (Association) Football Competition resulting in a draw - B.C's, 1 Goal; D/255, 1 Goal.	Cm Cm

Lieut.Colonel,R.F.A.(T).
COMMANDING 255TH (HIGHLAND) BRIGADE R.F.A.(T).

WO 44

51ᴿᴬ

Confidential

War Diary
of
255th Brigade R.F.A.
for January 1919

Army Form C. 2118.

WAR DIARY
or
INTELLIGENCE SUMMARY.
(Erase heading not required.)

Instructions regarding War Diaries and Intelligence Summaries are contained in F. S. Regs., Part II. and the Staff Manual respectively. Title pages will be prepared in manuscript.

Place	Date	Hour	Summary of Events and Information	Remarks and references to Appendices
ROEULX.	1919 1st to 31st Jan.		Brigade in billets at ROEULX. Demobilization of men and horses commenced. 3 officers, 88 men and 81 horses sent off. Educational training continued. In Divisional Football Competition (Rugby) 5th Royal Scots beat the Brigade 19 pts. to 0. (Association) 51st D.A.C. beat the Brigade 2 goals to 0.	T.D.
			J. Davidson — Lt.COLONEL, R.F.A.(T). Commanding 255th (Highland) Brigade R.F.A.(T).	

Army Form C.

WAR DIARY
or
INTELLIGENCE SUMMARY.
(Erase heading not required.)

Instructions regarding War Diaries and Intelligence Summaries are contained in F.S. Regs., Part II. and the Staff Manual respectively. Title pages will be prepared in manuscript.

51 Du / Vol 45

Place	Date	Hour	Summary of Events and Information	Remarks and references to Appendices
ROEULX.	1919. 1st. to 28th. Feby.		Brigade in billets at ROEULX. Demobilization of men and horses continued. 5.Officers 159 men and 11.horses sent off. In final of Brigade (Association) Football Championship "A" Battery beat "D" Battery - 1.goal to 0.- thereby winning the Brigade Cup. Educational training continued. A Silver Cup the gift of the Princess De Croy. "In remembrance of Armistice Days" was presented to the Brigade Officers on 16/2/19.	

Lieut-Col.R.F.A.(T)
Commanding 255th (High(Bde.R.F.A.(T)

Army Form C. 2118.

WAR DIARY
or
INTELLIGENCE SUMMARY.
(Erase heading not required.)

Instructions regarding War Diaries and Intelligence Summaries are contained in F. S. Regs., Part II. and the Staff Manual respectively. Title pages will be prepared in manuscript.

Vol 46

Place	Date	Hour	Summary of Events and Information	Remarks and references to Appendices
ROEULX.	1919. March 1st. to 23rd.		Brigade in Billets in Roeulx. All ammunition removed to Mons, and guns and wagons parked at Manage. Demobilization of men and horses continued. Orders received for Brigade to concentrate at MANAGE.	
	24th.		Personnel of Brigade moved to MANAGE. All equipment and stores ready for entraining. During month three Officers and sixty-one Other Ranks Demobilized. Two Officers and forty-two Other Ranks	
	to 31st.		dispatched to Army of Occupation. 451 Horses demobilized.	

Major, R.F.A.(T)

Commanding 255th (Highland) Bde. R.F.A.(T)

www.ingramcontent.com/pod-product-compliance
Lightning Source LLC
Chambersburg PA
CBHW081434160426
43193CB00013B/2277